Why God Needs
War and War Needs God

Why God Needs War and War Needs God

———⋙◉⋘———

MARK JUERGENSMEYER

OXFORD
UNIVERSITY PRESS

OXFORD
UNIVERSITY PRESS

Oxford University Press is a department of the University of Oxford. It furthers
the University's objective of excellence in research, scholarship, and education
by publishing worldwide. Oxford is a registered trade mark of Oxford University
Press in the UK and certain other countries.

Published in the United States of America by Oxford University Press
198 Madison Avenue, New York, NY 10016, United States of America.

First published as *God At War: A Meditation on Religion and Warfare*, 2020

First issued as an Oxford University Press paperback, 2025

Library of Congress Cataloging-in-Publication Data
Names: Juergensmeyer, Mark, author.
Title: Why God Needs War and War Needs God / Mark Juergensmeyer.
Description: New York, NY, United States of America : Oxford University Press, 2020. |
Includes bibliographical references.
Identifiers: LCCN 2019041492 (print) | LCCN 2019041493 (ebook) |
ISBN 9780190079178 (hb) | ISBN 9780197795804 (pb) | ISBN 9780190079192 (epub) |
ISBN 9780190079208
Subjects: LCSH: War—Religious aspects.
Classification: LCC BL65.W2 J83 2020 (print) | LCC BL65.W2 (ebook) |
DDC 201/.7273—dc23
LC record available at https://lccn.loc.gov/2019041492
LC ebook record available at https://lccn.loc.gov/2019041493

Paperback printed by Marquis Book Printing, Canada

MIX
Paper | Supporting
responsible forestry
FSC
www.fsc.org   FSC® C103567

Contents

War without Blood   89
Living with Competing Realities   93

Preface to the Paperback Edition

WHEN THE HEAD of the Russian Orthodox Church and a staunch ally of Vladimir Putin, Patriarch Kiril, proclaimed in his Easter Sunday sermon on March 5, 2022 that Russia's invasion of Ukraine was not just an ordinary conflict but one with "metaphysical significance," he was saying something fundamental about the role of religion in war. God was not just on Russia's side. The war itself was of transcendent proportions.

A similar notion appears to have been in the mind of Yahyah Sinwar, the leader of Hamas who gave the order for the attack on Israel on October 6, 2023. Sinwar is said to have compared himself with Saladin, the great warrior in Islamic history who liberated Jerusalem from Crusaders in 1187 CE, thereby placing himself in the pantheon of heroes in Islamic history.

A religious mission was also in the thinking of some right-wing members of Israel's cabinet as they pursued the war against Hamas in Gaza. Itamar Ben-Gvir, Israel's Minister of National Security and leader of the Jewish Power Party, subscribed to the idea of Eretz Israel, the God-given right of Israel to all of the land from the Jordan River to the Mediterranean Sea. He encouraged Palestinians fleeing the conflict to permanently leave Gaza and allow Jewish settlements to return.

In both the Ukraine and Gaza wars, religion has played a role, as it has in many other conflict situations around the world. But what kind of role? We know that often religious figures are brought in to bless soldiers before battle and that religious literature is full of images of warfare. It is clear that in these ways war needs God and religion needs war. But there is also a third option, when the idea of God and the idea of warfare are intertwined in one apocalyptic notion of cosmic war.

It is these ways of thinking about the relationship between religion and war that will be explored in this book. It will attempt to make sense of this dark relationship between violence and divinity and probe into the essential nature of both that makes them compatible with one another. What is it about the very essence of the idea of war that cries out for religious verification, and what is it about the character of the religious imagination that war is so easily assimilated into its world views?

This is a question that has haunted me over many years of studying religious-related violence in the rise of militant movements in virtually every major religious tradition. I have drawn upon my field work and conversations with activists in Iraq, Israel, Egypt, India, Japan, Myanmar, Sri Lanka, Philippines, the United States and elsewhere to understand the phenomena of religion and violence, and their connection, from the perspective of militants engaged in lethal struggles.

I sometimes describe their acts as incidents of religious violence, but I do not mean by that that religion causes violence. After all, the phrase "religious art" or "religious music" does not mean that religion causes art or music. Rather, I mean that religion is related to these things in some way. Just how they are related is what demands to be explored.

Strikingly, almost all militants whom I have met have described their support for violence as the justified acts of a defensive war. They also often describe it as a religious duty, a "neglected duty," as one Muslim writer has described jihad. This pattern of relationship between war and religion is what I want to understand. To put it in different terms, I have asked why God needs war and war needs God.

It is these questions that have dogged me over the years. I made an earlier attempt to answer them in a series of lectures given under the auspices of the Stafford Little Lectures at Princeton University in 2006. These lectures were to be published soon after, but at the time both the editor at Princeton University Press and I agreed that the ideas did not quite cohere, and that they were not ready for publication. So the project languished for some time until I received another opportunity to give a series of lectures on the topic, this time while serving as a visiting scholar at Münster University in Germany in 2018. By then I had a clearer sense of how the ideas fit together. In the years following the lectures I was able to expand on them and knit them together into this volume, first published in German and then in English. In writing this book, I've tried to preserve the cadence of conversation in which the lectures were given.

I am enormously grateful to Prof Detlef Pollack, the director of the Religion and Politics Cluster of Excellence at Münster University (formally known as the Westfälische Wilhem Universität Münster), and to members of the faculty who provided a lively and helpful discussion of many of the ideas advanced in this book. I also appreciated the editorial staff of Herder

Verlag, Frankfurt, publishers of the German version, and to the translator, Ulrike Berger, for rendering the book into readable German. Despite my German name and heritage, I am embarrassed to possess such little proficiency in my ancestors' native tongue.

The first English language version was shepherded into publication under the title *Why God Needs War and War Needs God* by the able staff at the New York offices of Oxford University Press. I am grateful to my editor, Cynthia Read, for her enthusiastic support for this volume and her wise counsel about it as we have worked together towards its publication. Remarkably she read and groomed every sentence in the volume, and the clarity and fluidity of the prose is in part due to her fine editorial hand. The persistence and support of my current editor at OUP, Theodore Calderara, has made this new edition possible.

In writing this book I was engaged in a five-year series of case studies of three militant religious-related movements—ISIS in Iraq, the Khalistan movement in India's Punjab, and the Moro movement in the Mindanao state of the Philippines. For research travel and support I am indebted to the Resolving Jihadist Conflicts Project of Uppsala University and its able director, Isak Svensson. Having studied the rise of violent religious movements over many years I wanted to look back at the major themes that animated them, and to understand how the movements ended. This project led to the publications of two books—this one on the concepts of religion and war, and its companion, *When God Stops Fighting, How Religious Violence Ends.*

Acknowledging all the assistance I have received in field research over thirty years would be exhausting, but I do want to give recognition to those who have assisted in my most recent field studies. In Iraq, I appreciated the arrangements facilitation of Prof Dilshad Hamad of Tishk University in Erbil, and Mushid Irwani, Founding Director of the Public Policy Institute, Erbil. For translation assistance I am grateful for Jeen Maltai in Dohuk, and Shahid Burhan Hadi in Suliamaniya, who also assisted in making arrangements. In the Mindanao region of the Philippines I appreciated the hospitality of the staff of Notre Dame University in Cotabato City, especially Fr Francis Zabala, President, and Sheila Algabre, Vice President for Administration; for his translating skills in Tagalog I'm deeply grateful to Collin Dvorak. In India's Punjab state, I am thankful for the assistance of three old friends: Mohinder Singh, Harish Puri, and Jagrup Singh Sekhon at Guru Nanak Dev University, Amritsar. For help in monitoring jihadi chat rooms and Twitter feeds, my thanks to two of my students, Saba Sadri and Mufid Taha. A host of other colleagues and former students have provided input along the way, including Barzin Pakandam, Jahan Ahmed, and Mona Kanwal Sheikh. Among my colleagues in the study of religion and violence I am particularly appreciative of the collegiality of Margo Kitts and the late Michael Jerryson.

As in all of my writings I am grateful for Sucheng Chan. Her own writings provide a model of conceptual clarity and textual fluidity that I have tried to emulate in more than fifty years that we have lived together. Perhaps someday I might achieve it.

Introduction

WHY DO WE THINK ABOUT WAR?

"THIS IS WAR," the Filipino man muttered sadly as we looked across the river at the ruins of the town of Marawi. Just weeks ago, in a five-month siege, Marawi had been flattened by a military action aimed at ridding the city of an ISIS-affiliated Muslim separatist movement. As we looked at it now, the city lay in ruins, marked with the scars of battle.

His comment startled me. I too was dismayed to see the extent of the destruction, but I knew that there was some controversy over who was responsible, who started it, and whether the military assault had been justified. Just as the cities of Mosul in Iraq and Raqqa in Syria were devastated in the effort to free them from the evil grip of the Islamic State of Iraq and Syria, this push to drive out ISIS rebels in the Philippine state of Mindanao had seen cities reduced to rubble. The liberating armies had to destroy the cities in order to save them.

I agreed that these were heavy-handed military operations. They might have been misguided. But were they war? My Filipino companion quietly repeated his observation, as if stating the obvious. What did he mean, and what did he see that I didn't?

I didn't live in Marawi, of course. He did. His family home was in the midst of the inner city, and he had lived through months of bombs and social dislocation. Now he was facing the specter of a ruined city across the river.

"There's nothing left," he told me, showing videos of what remained of his family home, taken several days earlier on his cell phone. He was right—there was only a pile of brick and stone rubble where once a multistory house had proudly stood.

Why God Needs War and War Needs God. Mark Juergensmeyer, Oxford University Press (2020)
© Oxford University Press. DOI: 10.1093/oso/9780190079178.001.0001

"My mother built that home with her sweat and toil," he said. She had worked for years as a domestic housekeeper in Saudi Arabia, carefully sending the earnings back to her family in the Philippines. Part of the money was for their college education. The rest was for the house in Marawi.

Though earlier he had been mildly sympathetic with the Muslim separatist movement in Mindanao, he told me, his attitude had hardened after the fighting. He knew now that they were in a state of war.

War—what a remarkable notion. It enabled him to see everything differently, through new eyes. He could no longer trust the government to do what was right; he increasingly saw it as an enemy that was beyond redemption. One could only fight and attempt to conquer it in a scenario of struggle that engulfed every aspect of the social world around him.

It is a strange way of thinking, this idea of war. It turns the world upside down. It creates demonic enemies out of competitors and brings normal civil activity to a halt. It animates ordinary people into a state of action, allowing them to kill and be killed, and cheer when the enemy—whose lives may not be all that different from theirs, men and women with families and duties and dreams—is destroyed, sometimes brutally so.

Yet history is full of war. Perhaps more perplexing, religion is full of it. Human creativity in general revels in it. It saturates popular culture— plays and movies, novels and television stories, comic books and computer games. It is the prevailing image in the minds of those who have undertaken acts of terrorism in recent years. And it is the idea that animates those who have launched their own wars on terrorism against it.

It is a powerful notion, war, and a puzzling one. For decades I have been studying the rise of religious violence around the world, including from groups like ISIS and Christian white supremacy movements that have been involved in acts of terrorism. Invariably war is central to their thinking. All of the activists with whom I have spoken eventually got around to the subject.

"Mr. Mark, there's a war going on," I was told by a jihadi militant who was imprisoned for his role in the 1993 bombing of the World Trade Center. "We knew it was war," a former fighter for ISIS told me when I talked with him in a prison in Iraq, "as soon as Saddam fell and the country was plunged into chaos and the Shi'a began oppressing us Sunnis." "We're at war," a Buddhist monk in Myanmar told me in justifying Buddhist attacks on the Muslim minority in his country. "We're in a war," a

Christian activist in the United States explained after the attack on the capital in 2021, adding, "It's not a metaphor, but a real war."

War is the central image in the worldview of virtually every religious extremist I have interviewed who was engaged in violent acts. Behind the moral justification of using violence in savage attacks are images of great confrontations, of war on a transcendent scale. My fascination with these notions of war has deepened into a profound curiosity about what war is and why it seems to emerge so spontaneously in response to situations of extreme shock, humiliation, and stress. I want to understand war, to understand how this template of the human imagination can transform our view of the world around us, and what religion has to do with it.

This book is about war—the idea of war, why it is so appealing, and why it is often associated with religion. I want to know why war needs religion and why religion needs war. What fascinates me is the idea of war—war in the mind. I am less interested in the actual use of lethal weapons than the worldview that makes that usage possible. I know that much has been written about the strategic decisions that go into warfare, about the cold calculations weighing economic benefits or political leverage against the cost of soldiers' lives, and about the political and moral justifications that allow for armed force in response to perceived threats. As important as these considerations are, though, they are not what I want to focus on in this book. What interests me is the quiet yearning for war that makes such calculations possible, the public acceptance of the notion that in some situations of social tension, war makes sense. It is this idea of war—this totalizing construct of the human imagination that absolutizes one's view of the world—that I want to explore.

It is this mentality that I am thinking of when I talk about war. It is not so much the act of warfare as the idea of it, the passion for war, the war worldview. The passion for war is not a rational thing. The conduct of military operations certainly involves a great deal of skill and rational calculation, but it seems to me that war—the idea of absolute conflict that precedes many but not all military acts—is almost an instinctual thing. It has much more to do with emotions—or a kind of inarticulate mental reflex—than with reasoned arguments. It is what I mean by "the war mentality," the way of seeing things in war-like terms.

In fact, the idea of war and the actions of military forces do not necessarily go together. There are police actions and humanitarian interventions, even on an international scale, that involve deadly force but are not regarded as war. A military raid undertaken to locate wrongdoers and bring them to justice is usually not thought of as war, but as a kind of police action. Representatives of the Philippine government told me that their military assault on the city of Marawi was not meant to be warfare but was simply an effort to capture members of a violent gang. When the FBI surrounded the Branch Davidian compound in Waco, Texas, on a fateful April day in 1993, their intention was not to kill the leader or burn alive the inhabitants of the compound. The FBI agents were not at war. But the members of the movement, trapped in what seemed to be a desperate situation and informed by biblical prophecies about the war at the end times, clearly saw things differently, just as the Muslim separatists in the Philippines saw the assault on Marawi differently. To them it was a salvo in a war in which they were a target. Militant actions are seen differently from different social perspectives. For those who accept that the motives of the US and Philippine governments were lawful in these cases, these are examples of police actions. For those who question the motives of those in authority and perceive a bellicose relationship between resistance groups and the government, Waco and Marawi were skirmishes in enduring wars. The application of military force and the idea of war are not necessarily identical.

Moreover the idea of war does not require constant military action. The Cold War involved various regional military encounters—in Cuba, Korea and Vietnam, for instance—but the overarching concept was greater than any of these specific military skirmishes.

For most of us who grew up in Europe or the United States in the era of the Cold War, in an odd way that global tension offered a reassuring view of the world. We knew who the good guys and the bad guys were, and we knew what to do about them. The decade after 1990 was one of uncertainty on a global scale. The "war on terror" announced by President George W. Bush in 2001 presented a new image of global war. Though not necessarily comforting, it imposed a template of meaning on international events. Again Americans knew who the good guys and the bad guys were, because everyone was either "for us or against us," as the president sternly insisted.

In public pronouncements and popular sentiment in the years that followed 9/11, the war on terror was seen to have been in some ineffable way blessed by God. In the United States, as elsewhere in the world when the sound of war drums is heard, the language of warfare is accompanied by religious rhetoric. Just as the Islamic terrorists proclaimed a holy war against America, the US response was also accompanied by a religious refrain, "God bless America." God, it seems, is always where the military action is.

This has been true throughout history. Whether it is the warfare of the Hebrew Bible or the great armies of the Hindu epics, God has marched alongside conquering armies. In our attempt to understand the idea of war, it is inevitable that we will also be trying to understand what God has to do with it. Why is religion so full of warfare, and why do wars always seem to employ God as a mercenary on both sides?

This book, then, is a meditation on war and religion. It is a reflection on the dark side of the human imagination, its capacity to deal with deep discomforts and profound anomalies in what strikes me as a horribly irrational way: by constructing a template of meaning that totalizes the differences between positions, Satanizes enemies, and gives moral sanction to the most hideous acts of destruction. What is this terrible thing called war? Why do we humans want it so? And why is God so often in command?

I

The Odd Appeal of War

"ARE WE AT WAR?"

These were the words with which the wife of a friend greeted me when they picked me up at the airport as I returned to California shortly after the attacks on September 11, 2001. I had been traveling on the East Coast, and it was only days after 9/11 when we met and she collapsed in my arms. Her voice trembled as she repeated the question.

"Are we at war?

Behind her fear was a profound sentiment. The implication was that an attack of the magnitude of 9/11 must be part of something on a more impressive scale than a rogue band of militant Muslims with a cleverly lethal scheme to perpetrate a dramatic symbolic attack.

Yet, in truth, what happened on 9/11 was basically that. The jihadi activists associated with Al-Qaeda were just a small gang of several hundred at most.[1] It was not a huge international army poised to challenge America's military power. September 11 was commonly likened to the attack on Pearl Harbor, but that is an oddly inappropriate parallel. They were both sudden, dramatic, and unexpected assaults, but the organizations behind them were vastly different: the military might of Japan was buttressed by an enormous army and the stature of an empire, while Al-Qaeda and its allies constituted a tiny network of perverse activists spread throughout the world, plotting their destructive designs through the internet. And Al-Qaeda had virtually no state support, aside from Osama bin Laden's Taliban hosts in Afghanistan.

The general public found it hard to fathom that such heinous acts as the attacks of September 11 could be accomplished by a small and relatively insignificant group. This misapprehension was magnified by the language of the media and by official pronouncements that spoke of the enemy in

Why God Needs War and War Needs God. Mark Juergensmeyer, Oxford University Press (2020)
© Oxford University Press. DOI: 10.1093/oso/9780190079178.001.0001

grand terms. The words signified that the hateful acts of bin Laden's small band of outlaws must signal something bigger than random terrorism. It is understandable, then, that my friend's wife instinctively thought it must be war.

Responding to Chaos

What does it take to make us think of war? In the case of the 9/11 attacks on the World Trade Center and the Pentagon, would my friend's wife have thought we were at war if things had played out differently—if the buildings were struck, for instance, but the Twin Towers did not fall? Would it have been war if the buildings collapsed, but it happened at night, when few people were killed and no cameras were there to record the event? What made this event, in the minds of many who witnessed it vicariously through televised images, so certainly an act of war?

I put these questions to a classroom of students when I returned to California shortly after 9/11. The discussion was lively, and at first there was little agreement.

"It was the magnitude of the event," one fellow intoned. He cited the importance of the World Trade Center and the Pentagon as public institutions, and the numbers of people who were killed. I pointed out that the buildings had been targeted before, in the 1993 attack by a jihadi group related to Al-Qaeda, and that event merited scarcely a shrug from the American populace. If the explosives were greater in magnitude and had been placed differently, both buildings would have collapsed immediately. The devastation would have been enormous. It would have killed far more than perished in 2001. Like a tree falling in the forest, the first tower would have toppled against the second, and both would have obliterated all of the other buildings in their shadow for blocks around. I calculated that as many as 200,000 people would have died.

"That would really have been war," the student responded. He went on to explain, however, that the relative lack of damage from what actually happened at the World Trade Center in 1993 disqualified it from being an act of war. September 11, 2001, was different, he said. The number of casualties and the dramatic visual impact of the event were good reasons for thinking of it as the onset of warfare.

Other students resisted the conclusion that it was simply the size of the event that made the difference. They noted that a natural disaster, such as a gas line explosion, or even the lone act of a crazy individual could have

killed as many people but would not have signaled a state of war. It had to
be an act that was rationally calculated, conducted by a significant force,
and deliberately aimed at us. The students noted the complexity of the
attacks and the fact that four airplanes were involved. All of this must have
taken an enormous amount of planning and coordination.

I pointed out that many of Al-Qaeda's previous activities were similarly orchestrated. The bombing of American embassies almost simulta-
neously in two different African countries in 1998, for example, reflected
a very sophisticated organizational scheme. So was the Bojinka plot, the
plan created by the Al-Qaeda operative Ramzi Yousef to bomb a dozen US
commercial airliners as they flew over the Pacific on one fateful day in the
early 1990s. Fortunately the plot was discovered before it could be carried
out. But it showed that Al-Qaeda had targeted America for some ten years
and yet the American public did not see itself at war.

"But September 11 was different," the students argued, "because it
worked." "And," one added, "because it was here."

For a moment there was silence, as if the students themselves were not
quite convinced by their own arguments. The points they made were all
good ones, but somehow none by itself seemed to have sufficient weight to
make a whole society think immediately and instinctively in terms of war.

"Besides," one of the women said, breaking the silence, "it was such a
crazy thing, those towers falling. It had to be war."

Now, it seemed to me, we were getting closer to the underlying issues.
The craziness of it all, the enormity of the impact on the public consciousness, the overwhelming sense of vulnerability and humiliation that was
the shared experience of most Americans at that time could only be explained by something as fundamental and fearsome as war.

But war requires two sides, I said. Who was the enemy? September
11 was greatly different from Pearl Harbor; the Japanese attack that drew
the United States into World War II involved a vast army commanded
by the authority of a nation-state in concert with its international allies.
War needs enemies. In this case it needed one of significant force to be a
worthy opponent of the largest superpower on earth.

I asked the students, "What if it turned out that the perpetrators of the
act were simply a ratty band of terrorists living in caves and connected to a
few comrades via email in different parts of the world? What if the enemy
in this case wasn't a significant force but a small but clever and very determined network of anti-American antiglobalization religious activists?
Would this still be war?"

The students appeared confused. I was describing a situation that they knew was at least to some extent true. If the enemy was only a tawdry band of miscreants, 9/11 would seem to be just a mindless act of terrorism and not a compelling case for war.

"Ah, but what about all their supporters?" a bright student asked, suddenly thinking of what might have been different about this case. "There's more to this than just Al-Qaeda," another said. And then yet another asked the definitive question: "Wasn't this really the first salvo in the war with the radical Muslim world?"

It was a chilling observation. It took the lid off a nasty little secret, that much of the American public blamed either the Middle East as a whole or the religion of Islam or both for implicitly supporting such acts of terrorism. This widely held but seldom expressed view was all the more disturbing in that it had the potential to be a self-fulfilling prophecy. In fact, soon after that classroom discussion, the United States was indeed at war with first one Muslim country, Afghanistan, and then another, Iraq, military actions that were justified in the minds of many by the war on terrorism but were widely perceived throughout the Muslim world as a war on Islam, to which many Muslims responded in kind.

The classroom discussion showed me that the idea of war is a powerful thing, based on one of the most potent of human emotions: the fear of uncertainty. It became clear to me that whatever else was behind the idea of war, it always began with a profound sense of public disorder. In the case of September 11, war was a response to an anomaly—a significant event that signaled a threat to our sense of order and public stability.

On the day of the attacks, however, the startled nation did not immediately think of war. A survey of the headlines that appeared in the afternoon editions of newspapers on September 11, 2001, shows that none of them described the attacks as acts of war. "U.S. Attacked," was the headline in the *New York Times.* "Terrorists Attack," said the *Washington Post* and the *Los Angeles Times.* "Infamy," and "A Day of Devastation," proclaimed others. Still other newspapers simply displayed a full-page picture of the burning towers with a phrase, such as "Terror Attacks" and "Who Did This?" The *San Francisco Examiner* printed a huge single word above the horrifying image of the burning towers: "Bastards."

Within the inner circle of the White House, there was apparently also uncertainty about how to describe the events. Secretary of State Colin Powell was in South America at the time. Though distraught over the attacks, his first reaction was to think of the terrorist networks that might be responsible for such a thing and how international intelligence agencies could be marshaled to locate them and bring them to justice. His boss, however, saw things in a different light. According to Bob Woodward's account, President Bush thought in terms of war.[2] Woodward described it as an immediate, almost visceral response.

That afternoon, when Bush appeared on television to comfort an anguished nation, he declared that the acts were committed not by a few misguided souls but by forces that three times in the short statement he described as "evil." It was also in this initial statement that he described America's response as "a war on terrorism." On the following day his assessment was raised a notch higher: the attacks were "more than acts of terrorism," the president said, "they were acts of war." Later that day the word "war" was used in conjunction with the attacks for the first time in the headlines of US newspapers, but it appeared in quotation marks, as the "act of war" described by Bush. That afternoon, on the Fox News Channel and other television outlets, Bush's phrase "the war on terrorism" was incorporated into the standard logo for news reports related to the attack and the US government's response, a logo that would be used for months and years following September 11 as one militant confrontation followed another. Often, though, the phrase was simplified to "the war on terror," indicating that it was not just a struggle against specific enemies but against the emotional response that their acts created in the minds of the public that was victimized by such attacks.

The way the event was framed, the way it was interpreted and understood as an act of war, was provided to the American public by its president. It is conceivable that if Colin Powell or Al Gore or someone else had been president, the event might have been described differently. It might have been portrayed as an awful but idiosyncratic act by a small group of misguided revolutionaries—an act that should be taken seriously but not considered war. Interpreting the events this way might have prevented the American public from quickly seeing the matter in terms that were grand, intractable, and absolute. But then again, it might not have. A calamity of such proportions as the collapse of the Twin Towers cried out for a large frame of reference to make it make sense. War provided that grand picture.

My hunch is that the woman who collapsed in my arms at the Santa Barbara airport and asked if we were at war was not just parroting the president. She was trying to make sense of things, and war provided a clarifying view. It gave an explanatory framework that made sense out of such a horrifying event as the massive destruction of public buildings. It might seem paradoxical given that war legitimizes killing and death, but the idea of war makes people feel more secure. Without war such a destructive event in the midst of ordinary life would leave individuals baffled and confused. Without war one's sense of vulnerability would be vastly increased—since one would be left without an understanding of why chaotic events happen and what can be done about them. The world is a dangerous place indeed if not just a major power but any little group with a grievance can do such things. In such a world, public order is highly unstable. The idea of war provides a potentially controllable view of the world. If the attacks were the orchestrated acts of a known and powerful foe, one would know how to deal with them. It is possible for people to imagine what caused the assault: an enemy with whom one is at war.

Imagining War

What I found striking about the response I met with at the airport after 9/11, and interesting about the American response in general, was how oddly similar it was to the worldview of the people behind the attacks. Like the Americans, the jihadi activists associated with the Al-Qaeda network felt under siege, victims of a great war that they could not see or understand. It took some mental gymnastics to imagine who the enemy was, and though initially not all agreed, many came around to bin Laden's perspective that it was the "far enemy" that was behind their loss of public morality and social meaning. It was America, and it was war.

I felt certain that this was the point of view of the jihadi activists because I had talked with one of them. Some years before 9/11, I had managed to worm my way into the prison precincts of Lompoc Federal Penitentiary and interview Mahmud Abouhalima, who had been convicted of conspiracy in the 1993 World Trade Center bombing. His network was intimately connected with the global jihadi movement, and in fact one of the masterminds of the operation was Ramzi Yousef, the nephew of Khalid Sheikh Mohammed, the activist identified in the official 9/11 Commission Report of the US government as being the main figure behind the 9/11 attacks. Both nephew and uncle were in prison, as was Abouhalima, whom *Time* magazine had featured on its cover as the main organizer of the 1993 World Trade Center bombing.

It took some effort to break into prison. I had to get the permission of the warden and Abouhalima himself. Though Abouhalima was eager to talk, his attorneys were hesitant, since they were still trying to get him a retrial and didn't want him to say anything that might implicate him. Eventually Abouhalima persuaded them that he would be cautious in his comments. My congressman at the time, Walter Capps, interceded on my behalf, persuading the warden to undertake the security measures necessary for me to visit, which I did on two occasions. After going through the lengthy security proceedings on my initial visit, I was placed in a cafeteria that had been emptied for the occasion. Guards stood nervously around the table where we were to meet, stationed there for my security, the warden told me, so that the prisoner would not try to grab me and take me hostage.

When Abouhalima appeared, he seemed less of a threat than one might have anticipated. I don't know exactly what people think a terrorist is supposed to look and act like, but whatever image of menace that might conjure, Abouhalima was not like that. He was tall and red-haired, unusual for an Egyptian, and he was also affable, eager to talk. There was nothing pious about him. He used mild profanities from time to time, "damn" this and "shit" that, and when I said that I was planning a trip to Sweden soon after our talk, he expressed interest in blond Scandinavian women.

In fact he portrayed nothing out of the ordinary until the conversation came to the topic of religion and politics. Then his face darkened and his eyes narrowed. He leaned over and spoke in an audible whisper.

"There's a war going on, Mr. Mark," he told me, his voice quiet but intense, his head lowered so that the guards who were standing nearby would not hear, adding, "and your government is the enemy."

He went on to say, "Someone should grab you by the shoulders, Mr. Mark." He let that sink in before repeating the point: "You need to be shaken awake." He sat back to see if I understood what he was saying.

Clearly this message was important to him. He was implying that I, and by extension most Americans, were blissfully unaware of a reality that seemed painfully obvious to him.

"You people are like sheep," Abouhalima continued, again repeating that we needed to be "shaken awake," jolted into awareness in order to understand what was really going on in the world.

It began to dawn on me what he was talking about. "Is this why people bomb buildings?" I asked.

He didn't answer directly, but he leaned back in his chair and smiled. "Well, now you know," he said. And after 9/11 all of us knew. We knew that they thought that the world was in a state of war.

Some years later I came to a similar conclusion after Anders Breivik had committed a hideous act of terrorism in Norway. On the night of June 22, 2011, I received an urgent message from colleagues in Oslo. They wanted my help to make sense of a curious manuscript that seemed related to a bombing in the downtown business district and a savage assault on a youth camp run by a liberal political party that advocated multiculturalism. Scores of young people had been shot at point-blank range; others died as they tried to swim to safety. It was one of those acts too horrible to imagine.

Why would anyone do such a thing? The manuscript my friends sent provided some answers. Breivik's 1,500-page rambling manifesto was all about war. He had given it the title *2083: A European Declaration of Independence.* The date is a reference to the four-hundredth anniversary of the battle at the gates of Vienna that kept the Ottoman army from turning central Europe into Muslim territory. The pictures that Breivik offered of himself dressed in military uniform as if a member of the Knights Templar evoked a period of warfare in which the Crusaders, the warriors of Christendom, were pitted against Muslim forces. Breivik imagined himself a modern-day incarnation of those Christian soldiers.

Though regarded as a lone-wolf killer, Breivik became the role model for other Christian terrorists, including Brenton Tarrant, who gunned down fifty-one Muslim worshippers at two mosques in Christchurch, New Zealand, on March 15, 2019. Tarrant's manifesto credited Breivik as his inspiration. On August 3, 2019, Patrick Wood Crusius drove ten hours to El Paso, Texas, to attack Hispanic people he regarded as unwelcome immigrants. His manifesto showed admiration for the Christchurch shootings, and like Tarrant and Breivik, he thought of himself as a warrior in a great battle for white supremacy.

Once again I was confronted with a central question: Why war? What were the circumstances that led the participants to see their predicament in the guise of warfare? And why was war the common reflexive perspective for activists related to every religious tradition—not only Muslims like Abouhalima and Christians like Breivik and Tarrant, but Jews, Hindus, Buddhists, and Sikhs. Why did they all think of war, and what did religion have to do with it?

This question was on my mind when I went to Baghdad some months after the US invasion and occupation of Iraq. By then a Muslim resistance movement had sprung up. It was more than a protest against occupation; it involved organized militia attacks. The American authorities seemed surprised when large segments of the population, especially Sunni Muslims in western Iraq, failed to show their appreciation for being liberated from Saddam Hussein and instead attacked the occupying US forces with a vengeance.

Our hosts in Baghdad arranged a meeting with one of the leaders of the Association of Muslim Clergy from Al Anbar province, which was at the center of the armed resistance. I was joined by my colleague, Professor Mary Kaldor of the London School of Economics, who had arranged the trip.

We met at a mosque that had been one of Saddam's favorites and was now occupied by the Al Anbar Sunni clerical association. It was called the Mother of All Battles Mosque, named in honor of Saddam's claimed great victory in the Gulf War against the Americans and their allies after his invasion of neighboring Kuwait. Appropriately enough, the mosque named to honor Saddam's battle against the Americans would now be occupied by clergy who were supporters of new battles against Americans.

"Why Americans?" I asked the leader of the Association of Muslim Clergy from Al Anbar province. "Why are they under attack?"

"This is war," the cleric said, as if stating something obvious.[3] He seemed to think that the question needed no more response than that, and he went on to cite many of the grievances of the Sunni Arabs with respect to the military occupation. It struck me as odd that these grievances, as understandable as they were, did not amount to the life-and-death confrontation of war.

But later the Muslim leader talked about the social disruption at the time of the American military invasion. He said that initially there was a wait-and-see attitude. The Iraqis did not know what to expect, and they were used to authoritarian rule. They had survived Saddam and tolerated the British, so they could abide the American regime if they thought it was just. But almost immediately they saw images of massive looting and public disorder as Saddam's dictatorial regime disintegrated into chaos. As much as they abhorred Saddam, the chaos was worse. It was war.

It is a remarkable idea, the idea of war. It came over Iraq like a cloud that poisoned the process of peaceful transition to a democratic state. It descended into the thinking and attitudes of Iraqis months and years after the end of the initial assault—after the battles of the invasion were over and after Americans had congratulated themselves on "a job well done." Gradually the idea insinuated itself into the minds of many average Iraqis, who began to see the American-led coalition forces as more than just an irritating occupying presence. They became enemies in a global war.

In an interesting way, this image of warfare was the mirror response to the war on terror, the patriotic militancy after 9/11 that brought US troops to Iraq in the first place. Many of the young American men and women who volunteered to fight did so in a mood of revenge, of wanting to retaliate against those who had attacked the World Trade Center and brought such startled grief to their country. No matter that Saddam had nothing to do with Al-Qaeda or 9/11. In their minds they were repaying the Middle East for the suffering it had brought to America. They were replicating the thinking of those Muslim militants who plotted the terrorist attack, who were attempting to repay the United States for the suffering they imagined it had brought to those who lived in the Middle East. War begat war.

The wheel of warfare had come full circle. The simmering resentment over American power and influence in the Muslim world had crystallized into a sense of warfare. A decade of sporadic jihadi terrorist attacks finally struck home on September 11, 2001—or rather September 12, when the US president announced that he had adopted the jihadis' worldview and, like them, saw the world at war. This led to real war in the US military action in Afghanistan weeks later. The American public's gnawing fear of a vague international threat of global jihadi war would become a major element in the popular support for the invasion of Iraq. This invasion and the bungling American occupation that followed added fuel to the fires of Muslim extremism throughout the Middle East. It facilitated the rise of ISIS, which became the impetus for another US military action to destroy the vicious regime of the Islamic State. This opened a new theater of conflict that culminated in the 2018 destruction of the cities of Mosul and Raqqa and gave rise to ISIS-inspired terrorist attacks from Manhattan to Paris, from Mindanao to Sri Lanka. Again, war begat war.

How did this come to pass? Why did this way of thinking about the world—a world embroiled in war—seem on both sides to be so natural, so inevitable, so appealing? What is the odd attraction of war?

The Ubiquity of War

Trying to discern why war is so appealing, I turned to the cultural images of war. They are ubiquitous. Truly war is everywhere, in our art and stories, legends and myths, sports and games. This is not just a response to specific enemies but in some deep way a response to the human condition. It is as common as the movies that populate the neighborhood Cineplex and the video games that mesmerize teenage boys. These images are compelling not just to incipient terrorists but to everyone who is fascinated by and engaged with them, which is virtually everyone, from the kid next door to families in front of the evening television shows, readers of fiction, and devout parishioners in their weekly worship services. What is war doing everywhere?

Humans are social animals, and our main activities are aimed at creating societies that are peaceful, orderly, and just. Differences are negotiated or brought to arbitration or subject to the rule of law. Ordinarily we strive to get along with one another, so why should the idea of war be even remotely attractive? Since the orderly adjudication of differences is the hallmark of civil society, why would we want to imagine a situation in which humans are objects and those who differ from us are aliens to be destroyed? Yet it is precisely this alternative to normal life—not just a little bit different but completely different, in fact its very opposite—that images of war provide.

Though many video games, such as Minecraft and Tetris, are creative and nonviolent, the ones that capture the attention of many boys and young men in particular are all about war. These include Grand Theft Auto, which is about urban gang warfare, Fortnite, Counter-Strike, League of Legends, World of Warcraft, and Call of Duty: Modern Warfare, each of which has garnered sales in the tens of millions. When Fortnite was launched in 2018 it quickly was sold to 3.8 million players around the world and Counter-Strike sold tens of millions of copies after it was created in 2000. A later iteration of the game is Counter-Strike: Global Offensive; in mid-2018 its website claimed that over ten million players were actively engaged with the game each month.[4]

Fortnite and Counter-Strike are online games, meaning that they can be played on any computer linked to the internet rather than on the consoles that are found in video arcades and on personal game stations. (The makers of Counter-Strike also produce a console version of the game, which is less successful.) They are role-playing games, which are vastly more popular than those that, rather like chess, are primarily about calculating an effective military strategy. In role-playing games, players enter into the action and become fighters engaged in combat. They are required to choose roles—in the case of Counter-Strike they may be either terrorists or counterterrorists—and wage war against each other. The premise of Fortnite is that zombies have taken over the world; the player cannot choose to join them but rather must take a role and strategize to help destroy them. In both games the enemies have no humanity or personality but are simply objects to be destroyed. Since the enemies in Fortnite are zombies and therefore subhuman, or even counterhuman, one need not feel any moral guilt about annihilating them.

To understand the vast appeal of these games, I interviewed a small group of high school boys from various locations in California who attended a precollege summer event at my university. They affirmed what already seemed obvious: that the audience for these games tend to be middle-class males like themselves who often became hooked on video games during junior high school and found it an enormously time-consuming activity well into their college years. Though Fortnite is making an effort to lure female players by presenting images of strong and competent female figures in the games, the audience for war games is still mostly male. My informants said that some of their friends played these or similar games for at least six hours a day, every day of the week.

What did they like about them? I asked. Predictably, they said, "It's fun." Pressed to explain why young men like themselves would choose to spend a vast amount of solitary time playing war games to the exclusion of social interaction with family and friends, they said that it presented a clearly defined world, with sudden and unpredictable dangers that they could navigate and control. There were good guys and bad guys, and with luck the good guys won. And if not, there was always another game.

When I tried to probe into why the violent aspect of the games was appealing, the young men insisted that they didn't think of the enemy as a person but as an object to be destroyed. Would the game be just as compelling if objects or abstract symbols replaced the images of people? No, they confessed, it would not. They "wanted to see blood." Grudgingly they accepted the fact that part of the fun was vicarious violence. During the time that they were playing the game, all of the complexities of civility were removed. So was the patina of propriety. The game presented a social order of fearful chaos and suspenseful danger in which there were enemies and friends, and only by skill and close attention could they survive.

In a curious way, they felt, the world of these video games was a deeper and more honest presentation of social reality than they experienced in the niceties of orderly life. While playing the games they could act on their instincts, unchecked by civility, and be rewarded for their cunning. At their age, I recalled, the world of a high school student seemed precarious, with lots of unknowns and meaningless restraints. In the games they could navigate such a world with dexterity and freedom. And if it didn't work out—well then, there was always another game.

Portrayals of warfare are also ubiquitous in literature and sometimes as adventurous and thrilling as in Fortnite, Counter-Strike, and Grand Theft Auto. But often not. The search for the truth about war is the main point of one of the most successful novels about warfare, Ernest Hemingway's *For Whom the Bell Tolls*. The protagonist, Robert Jordan, is lured into joining the international cadre fighting the Fascist regime in the Spanish Civil War. At first it was like "taking part in a crusade," Jordan recalls. Later he thinks his romantic enthusiasm for warfare to be "as difficult and embarrassing to speak about as a religious experience," but he also insists that his involvement in it was indeed "authentic." Much of the allure of warfare is being immersed in a total experience. "It gave you a part in something that you could believe in wholly and completely," Jordan recalls. It is a way of accepting the world and one's role in it totally and without compromise, and it also offers a new community, a band of brothers that replaces the kinship network of family. In war, Jordan recalls, "you felt an absolute brotherhood with the others who were engaged in it."[5]

My interviews with former soldiers revealed thinking that was strikingly similar to Jordan's in Hemingway's fictional story. A former student who served several tours of duty in Afghanistan and Iraq told me that he cringed every time someone said to him, "Thank you for your service." He explained, "We were only trying to survive, to protect each other." He was an Army Ranger often placed in difficult battle situations manning a bazooka missile and at other times required to kick in doors and take villagers off for interrogation. Though he came to question the motives of the US military presence in the region, and later joined the movement of Veterans Against the War, he felt strangely attracted to the camaraderie of military life and admitted to me that if he had to do it over again—despite his feelings about US policy in the region—he would. He told me he never felt more alive than in war.

The hero in Hemingway's novel experiences the same kind of fascination with war. Throughout the novel Jordan continually questions and reevaluates his understanding of war, and with this comes a loss of innocence. For Hemingway, war is a metaphor for the rough, beating heart of life, a terrible but honest appraisal of existence that always lies beneath the superficialities of the normal social order. To think about war is to think about the battle for survival, the meaninglessness of high-minded virtues, the withering barrage of assaults on the self—both physical and emotional—and the futility of struggle in the face of the ultimate victor, death. Jordan goes to war to fight for what he believes is a morally just cause—"a crusade"—but as the novel continues, his conception of a just cause is eroded. For much of the novel he is confused. He attempts to reconcile his romantic image of warfare with the gritty reality. Even the idea of an enemy seems pointless; he is faced with opponents who seem in many ways like himself, motivated ultimately not by a grand purpose but, like my former student who fought in Iraq, by the simple human will to survive.

The classic Hindu epic the *Mahabharata* also finds in the images of warfare insights about human existence. The *Mahabharata* has existed in the form that most people in India know it today for about two millennia. The other classic epic, the *Ramayana*, dates from about the same time. These great stories about Krishna and Rama, the two main avatars of the god Vishnu, are the mainstay of popular Hindu religiosity. Television series based on the epics have been among the most popular ever viewed in India; when the series were first aired, all traffic and commerce ceased during the Sunday evening hour when they were on. Even though the graphics were primitive and the acting melodramatic, the ancient stories were mesmerizing, showing the persistence of their narrative power.

Both of the epics are about warfare, grand warfare, often vividly portrayed in calendar art featuring the goriest of battles. Paintings in brilliant primary colors show arrows filling the air, blood spurting from wounded bodies, and severed limbs lying mangled on the ground. The god-heroes are spotless and gleaming, carried in golden chariots through the fray.

In the battles of the *Mahabharata* the combatants are divided into the good guys and the bad guys, as battles always are. Yet the struggle is not simply a Manichaean cosmic conflict between good and evil. The motif that runs through these mythic scenes of warfare is the theme of us versus them, the known versus the unknown. In the Bible and in the *Ramayana*, the enemies are often foreigners from the shady edges of known civilization, places like Canaan and Philistia in the Bible, and Lanka in the Ramayana. These foes often embody the conceptual murkiness of their origins; they represent what is chaotic and uncertain in the world, including those things that defy categorization altogether.

In the *Mahabharata*, however, war is waged between sets of cousins, though one set is portrayed as more honorable than the other. The idea of chaos is embodied not so much by an inhuman evil foe as by the battle itself. It is the wickedness of warfare that the battle depicts, as the mythic figure Arjuna observes at the outset of his encounter with Lord Krishna on the battlefield.[6] To fight in such a circumstance is to assent to the disorder of this world, although the contestants know that in a grander sense this disorder is corrected by a cosmic order that is beyond killing and being killed.

Such is the message of Lord Krishna in his address to Arjuna at a critical moment of battle. Arjuna wonders aloud why he is going to war with his cousins. He knows that the outcome of the battle will be either his killing them or their killing him. Either way, it is a messy business. He wonders what the point of this could possibly be. As luck would have it, Arjuna's chariot driver just happens to be Lord Krishna in disguise. He hears Arjuna's plaintive questioning and gives an extensive reply—which we know as the Hindu scripture called "The Song of the Blessed One," the *Bhagavad Gita*.[7]

Krishna provides several answers to Arjuna's question "Why war?" One is that there are roles in life for every kind of activity, and this lot has fallen to him. Another answer is that the soul survives even though the physical body may be destroyed, so death is not to be feared. The most interesting answer is one of the last: that in this life warfare is inevitable. One cannot avoid or escape it, as the ascetics in their mountain caves foolishly believe. Rather, to be in life is to be involved in the messiness of life's struggles.

The *Bhagavad Gita, From Whom the Bell Tolls,* and popular games like Fortnite and Counter-Strike show that war gives clarity to situations of madness. They all portray life's chaos, yet the depiction of this mortal messiness as battle gives it structure and meaning.

There may be no more eloquent statement of the terror and energy of warfare than Pablo Picasso's mural depicting an episode in the Spanish Civil War that took place in the town of Guernica. What the painting *Guernica* says about war—in its silent screams, its broken daggers, its contorted horses, and its terrible illumination of light—is that war is indeed a kind of hell. It is everything that civil society is not. Where normal society offers understanding and accommodation of differences, war provides absolute enemies and either-or dichotomies. Where ordinary communities go to great lengths to protect life, blood in a time of war is cheap and readily spilled. Where civil order respects law and the familiarity of routine, the theaters of war are madhouses of confusion and desperate efforts to survive in the midst of massacre. War is the very antithesis of civilization. And yet Picasso's riveting portrayal of this anti-order is itself a kind of order, literally putting a frame around chaos.

Living with Chaos

The English word "war" comes from the Old English *werra*, which means "confusion" or "chaos" and is probably related to the old Saxon word *werran*, "to bring into confusion." It is the basis of the French word for war, *guerre*. A related Old German word, *wers*, "mixture," is behind the English word for extreme disorder, "worst." Amusingly, it is also the basis for the German word for sausage, *wurst*, savory tubes that contain a mixed-up assortment of meats and other ingredients. War, like sausage, encompasses a mixed-up state of things.

It is interesting that the Germans themselves did not evolve a word for war based on *werre*. Instead, the Germans use *krieg*, based on another early word, one that means "striving," a word with the same meaning as the Arabic *jihad*. The old Latin word for war, *bellum*, did not survive in common European usage probably because it sounds like the Italian word *bella*, "beautiful," and there is very little beauty in war. The word *bellum* may have originated in an earlier word for bravery and may have been related more to a situation of battle than to a state of war. The various words for war reflect our diverse feelings about it. On the one hand it signals bravery and striving; on the other it portrays not just military actions but also the state of confusion that the word *werra* denotes.

One way of thinking about war is to see it as a way of imagining and struggling with chaos. War helps to make sense of chaos. This means that as horrible as war is for its victims, it is first and foremost an idea. It is war in the mind long before it is war in the finger on the trigger of a gun. Though war implies the threat of violence and justifies the use of it, war does not require violence. A society can be gripped with the mindset of war even when no military action is undertaken. One can have a warring attitude without ever firing a shot.

War—or rather the process of thinking in terms of warfare—begins with chaos, with the dark fear of uncertainty and confusion. The shocking images of the attack on the World Trade Center created such fear, but so did the slowly growing conviction that society was unraveling and no one was in control, as the Sunni Arabs observed in Iraq after the US invasion of their country. It starts with an attempt to make sense out of a senseless situation, something that deeply threatens one's sense of order. By "deeply threatening," I mean something capable of destroying meaning itself. War is the response to the perception of imminent danger, not just personal physical danger but an existential threat—the sense that even if one is not killed, an essential sense of identity and meaning will be lost.

In an interesting moment in my prison interviews with Mahmood Abouhalima, he recalled that he had turned to a jihadi perspective at a moment in his life when he felt that his "world was falling apart." What he had in mind was not just what he regarded as the political oppression of the Mubarak regime in his native Egypt—a dictatorship that Abouhalima saw as propped up by the economic and military power of the United States—but also something more personal. After leaving Egypt and joining the Muslim resistance movement in Soviet-controlled Afghanistan and then living in the West—first in Germany and then in Brooklyn and Jersey City in the United States—he succumbed to the easy temptations of sex, alcohol, and drugs, he said, and adopted the superficial lifestyle that he imagined all Europeans and Americans inhabited. But then he renewed his faith in Islam. He told a parable popular in the Middle East to describe this return to religion. A lion that had been adopted by sheep did not realize that he wasn't actually a lamb until one day at the water hole he saw his image reflected on the surface of the water and realized what he really was. "And that, Mr. Mark," Abouhalima told me, "is what Islam showed me: that I'm not a lamb but a lion."

It was not just Islam that Abouhalima had accepted, but the jihadi version of it. To be true to the faith meant not only accepting its tenets but engaging in the struggle with its enemies. That meant war, specifically war against the enemies of Islam, a category that included the United States. He heard this call to arms when he experienced a deep sense of fear about the loss of his own integrity and the uncertainty of the social order. It is true that individuals often have such feelings for a variety of personal reasons, but when others share this feeling that the social order is in danger of collapsing, it this can be the first step toward thinking that an alien enemy is behind the upheaval.

So war begins with a feeling. It is the anxiety that something is terribly wrong, not just in one's personal life but in the wider world. It is the experience of a social anomaly—something out of place in the social order. More than that, it is a social anomaly that is personally threatening, that has the potential for total destruction on both individual and social-cultural levels. Abouhalima felt personally upset by what he perceived as political and social disarray in Egypt and the Middle East. Because the feeling that the "world was falling apart" had the potential to damage or even destroy his personal life, he experienced it as an emotional as well as a political problem. When individuals feel a rising sense of social fear, the experience is compounded by their interactions with friends and neighbors who confirm their own worst suspicions about the dangerous trends in the world around them. It is at this moment that the idea of war begins to make sense.

What happens next? Here is where the details in the notion of war began to evolve. It is one thing to feel fear, to sense that the world is going awry, and quite another to take the next step and understand the fearful chaos as part of a scenario of conflict. In the face of a hideous and deeply threatening reality, the idea of war is comforting. It comes as a moment of insight and a kind of mental relief. The image of war is the solution to a conceptual problem. It explains why terrible things are happening in the world.

Chris Hedges, a thoughtful American journalist, reflecting on his experiences as a war correspondent, writes that war is "a force that gives us meaning."[8] Hedges goes on to chronicle the horrors of the reality of war and concludes that war is seductive because it provides both intellectual and emotionally satisfying responses (however illusory) to difficult situations on both personal and social levels. As starkly different as this war world is from our own world, we recognize it in a haunted, fearful way. It is that aspect of reality that we usually do not want to confront or even admit into our consciousness. It is a world that all of us know exists only slightly out of our range of vision. But it is always there—a distant glimpse of the reality that ordinarily we would like to pretend is beyond our imagination. But imagine it we do, because we cannot deny its powerful existence. Every day reminds us of the untidy chaos that intervenes to contradict justice and law and the inevitability that our own realities will terminate in the mystery of death.

War is attractive, then, in an awful sort of way. It forces us to look at the blemished, fecal, decaying reality of life that we do not want to confront and yet do. It is appealing to think about because it presents an arresting image of a reality that we feel we must somehow try to understand, related to but ultimately different from our ordered lives. It also offers a way of domesticating those images, transferring them from horror to a reaffirmation of life; it portrays disorder in a form that confronts it, contains it, and ultimately hopes to destroy it.

This explains why images of war are fascinating and why we cannot turn away from them any more than we can avoid staring at a horrible traffic accident at the edge of the road. But it does not quite explain the appeal of actually undertaking warfare rather than simply dwelling on images of it. Why do we sometimes not only become engaged in the fantasy as individuals but actually participate in a shared social perception of war?

I would like to suggest that the process of thinking is the same. The same factors that conduce to making war appealing in one's individual imagination are what make war collectively appealing in dealing with an intransigent social reality. In both cases the idea of war takes root in a disturbing awareness of deep disorder. War is a way of thinking about this chaos, giving it a dichotomous structured order, and imagining a way in which the confusion can be made clear and the demons of danger conquered. The only difference between symbolic war on an individual level and war embraced as a social attitude and as public policy is the level on which the angst of disorder is felt—whether it is a fear experienced in solitude or a threat shared by members of a social group. In either case, war is a way of dealing with something that profoundly challenges the foundations of our rational existence. This is why war, whether as a fantasy or as an actual military engagement, is an exercise of imagination. It is a way of thinking and living through chaos in order to break free from the fear that it will become an all-consuming fire.

Notes

1. Documents seized in the raid on Osama bin Laden's compound in which he was captured and killed in 2011 indicate that in 2002 there were 170 members of the movement. David Blair, "Secret Osama bin Laden Files Reveal al Qaeda Membership," *The Telegraph*, May 3, 2012, https://www.telegraph.co.uk/news/worldnews/northamerica/usa/9243503/Secret-Osama-bin-Laden-files-reveal-al-Qaeda-membership.html.

2. Bob Woodward, *Bush at War* (New York: Simon and Schuster, 2002).

3. From my interview with Sheik Muhammad al-Kubaisi, deputy secretary general of the Association of Muslim Clergy, Baghdad, May 7, 2004.

4. This statement may be found on *Counter-Strike* (blog), http://blog.counter-strike.net/. Valve Software, a division of Sierra Software Corporation, owns the patent to Counter-Strike.

5. Ernest Hemingway, *For Whom the Bell Tolls* (New York: Charles Scribner's Sons, 1940), chapter 18, 221.

6. *Bhagavad Gita*, chapter 1, verse 45.

7. *Bhagavad Gita*, chapter 2, verses 19–34.

8. Chris Hedges, *War Is a Force That Gives Us Meaning* (New York: Anchor Books, 2002).

2

War as an Alternative Reality

"THOSE WERE THE DAYS," the old rebel told me, reminiscing about the peak period of the Sikh rebellion against the Indian government in the 1980s. I had interviewed some of his fellow militants in the Indian state of Punjab years before, when the movement was still active, and later I returned to the Punjab to assess how the scars from those years had healed.

In Surjit Singh's case, they hadn't. He was still bitter about all that happened following the collapse of the movement and the end of the violence in the 1990s. But when he recalled the glory days of the movement, his face lit up. Clearly those years were the high point of his life.

I met with Singh in the dusty village of Sultanwind, several miles outside the Punjab city of Amritsar. It was where he was raised and had lived most of his life. In the 1980s it came to be known as "Little Khalistan" because it was in the center of the maelstrom of militant activity associated with the movement to create a Khalistan, a separate Sikh state. For over ten years the Indian government and its armed police battled the militant rebels, who were led by several organizations that were structured as military units.

It was a war, and a bloody one at that. The militants kidnapped police, politicians, and journalists and often strangled them or slit their throats. Buses traveling through the region were captured and their passengers attacked and killed. An Air India jetliner flying out of Canada was blown up midflight. A car bomb was set off outside the Punjab state secretariat, killing the chief minister. For their part, the Indian armed police seemed to match the brutality, simply executing suspected terrorists in extrajudicial killings that were often reported as "police encounters." Over the years thousands were killed on both sides.

Why God Needs War and War Needs God. Mark Juergensmeyer, Oxford University Press (2020)
© Oxford University Press. DOI: 10.1093/oso/9780190079178.001.0001

All of the young men in his generation were involved in the struggle, Singh told me. His older brother, Kuldip, was a rising star in the movement, and his buddies looked up to him as if he were a football hero. Kuldip joined one of the central organizations in the militant movement, the Babbar Khalsa, as his younger brother Surjit (not his real name) looked on with admiration.

Though he was still a teenager, Surjit began joining Kuldip in some of the nonviolent activities of the movement. They helped to sponsor a protest march against what they felt was Pakistan's unfair exploitation of water from the Sutlej River, which deprived Sikh farmers in the Punjab their full allotment. Kuldip began listening to the teachings of Jarnail Singh Bhindranwale, the key figure in the Khalistan movement, and spreading his message of the unity of rural Sikhs—mostly from the landowning Jat caste—in opposition to what he described as the oppression of the Indian government.

Although he realized that his brother was secretly involved in suspicious activities, Surjit claimed that he was unaware of the details. The Punjab police, however, assumed that both brothers were engaged in nefarious actions and arrested Surjit along with Kuldip; both were soon released, however, since the police did not have firm evidence against them.

In 1986 the police arrested Kuldip again. According to Surjit they tortured his brother for a month before putting him to death. The police began to pursue Surjit as well, assuming he was equally culpable in whatever crimes they suspected Kuldip of committing. He went into hiding. Later that year, when he was twenty-one years old, he became fully committed to the movement. He joined the Khalistan Commando Force, which was headquartered in Sultanwind, and spent the next six years in the movement, moving from village to village under the cover of night to avoid detection by the police.

Eventually he was captured. It was now the 1990s and the movement was falling apart. Villagers were no longer willing to shelter the rebels, and the Punjab police, under the strong command of Director General K. P. S. Gill, were offering a bounty for any militant who was rounded up, dead or alive. Surjit was captured and for the next eight years waited in prison to stand trial in one case after another. He was accused of having been a hit man who killed police, informants, and their families. The evidence, however, was deemed insufficient for conviction, and eventually he was released. Since then, however, his life has been restricted. His passport was taken away so he cannot travel outside the country; he is unable to receive government loans or benefits; and he continues to be under surveillance.

When I asked why he had joined the movement in the first place, he hesitated before answering. The police treated him as the enemy, he said, so he reacted in kind. He thought he was doing something good for his community. Besides, everyone was joining the movement in those days, and he wanted to impress his brother.

He fell silent, as if he were looking for some other, more basic explanation. "It was what we did," he finally said, as if there had been no other option.

This response was typical, I was told by Jagrup Singh Sekhon, a political scientist at Guru Nanak Dev University in Amritsar who has studied scores of ex-militants in the Punjab. "They were just caught up in the moment."

In Surjit Singh's telling, he did not come to the war as much as the war came to him. The sense of struggle, the war worldview, descended on Sultanwind and other Punjab villages like a dark cloud, engulfing everything. Without quite wanting or asking for it, they were at war.

Understanding What War Is

How can we make sense of what happened to Surjit Singh? When war came to Sultanwind, what was it, and how did it change things? As a professional academic, my inclination is to turn immediately to the literature, to understand how other scholars have framed a subject. However, in the case of war this tactic doesn't much help.

I was trained in two different disciplines, political science and theology. Both talk about war, but quite differently. It may seem that I was something of an overachiever, having acquired two master's degrees and a PhD in addition to my BA. But in truth this was the result of indecision and bad planning on my part. I had initially wanted to become a Protestant minister, so my first choice for graduate school was theology. I chose Union Theological Seminary in New York City, which was and still is a powerhouse of scholarship in religious studies.

It was at Union that I realized I was much more interested in thinking about religion and studying it than preaching it, so my mind turned to other graduate programs. After graduating from seminary, though, I spent two years abroad in India. I became fascinated with the way religion in that ancient culture was intimately intertwined with the social and political aspects of life. So when I returned to the United States, I applied and was admitted to a graduate program in political science at the University of California at Berkeley, to study religion and politics. (The mid-1960s were an auspicious time to be in Berkeley for all sorts of political and cultural reasons, but that is quite another story.)

In the PhD program in political science one much-discussed book at that time was *Man, the State and War*, by Kenneth Waltz.[1] It continues to be one of the most articulate statements about war from a political science perspective. Waltz surveys a wide range of classical theories about war and groups them into three categories, which he calls "images" of war. One is on an individual level, by which he means not only the penchant for fighting, which he thinks is endemic to human nature, but also the ability of individual leadership—a Napoleon, say, or a Hitler—to rally the citizenry and lead a society into war. The second image is on the level of state policy, which posits that wars are started in order for states to acquire something or to make up for some internal deficiency by solidifying social support. The third image is international, the arena of concern that interests Waltz the most. Here he sees the cause of war in the anarchic world system, where there is no global power, nothing to check the impulse of one state to impose its will on others.

There is no question that warfare is often part of the strategy of international politics and can be used and manipulated by skillful political leaders. But if this is all that war is—an extension of political calculations by means of military force—then every instance of war would have to demonstrate that the benefits exceeded the costs, or at least that those involved in the decision to go to war expected that this would be the case. It does not explain why state actors think in war terms even when it does not make rational sense, as when US leaders proclaimed a "war on terror" against an ill-defined enemy after 9/11. And it does not explain why nonstate movements and groups would adopt an attitude of war even when there are overwhelming odds against them.

The Khalistan movement was one of these nonstate movements, so the war that Surjit Singh discovered does not quite fit into any of Waltz's themes. And the political scientist does not help much in understanding individuals' perspectives and how they see the world at war. Waltz's view is largely from the top down, seeing war as a matter of state policy. It is a thoughtful study of the role that war plays in the international relations of states, but it does not help much in understanding the appeal of war to those who are lured into it, even as spectators.

So I turned to theology for answers, thinking it would offer a more sympathetic perspective. In some ways this was true, but only because theology focuses on the moral dimensions of warfare. Traditional theological thinking about war is still, like Waltz, concentrated on the idea of warfare as a matter of state policy.

At Union Theological Seminary I was privileged to study with Reinhold Niebuhr, one of the foremost theologians of the twentieth century. He had been a pacifist in his early years and a socialist, but with the rise of Stalin and then Hitler he realized that the massive violence of powerful state actors such as these could not in good conscience be left unchecked. In a pivotal essay published as a short book, *Why the Christian Church Is Not Pacifist*, Niebuhr argued that the just war tradition of Christianity applied to contemporary cases where violent powers needed to be contained.[2] The just war theory says that killing is bad, war is bad, but there are moments when you have to apply some force in order to keep a greater amount of force from happening. The force applied should be proportional at most, authorized by a just authority, and as swift and sure as "a surgeon's knife."[3]

I greatly admire Niebuhr's thinking and respect the ethical conundrum that arises when trying to decide the appropriate degree of force necessary to confront the violence of evil forces. When it comes to understanding what war means to Surjit Singh, however, alas, Niebuhr, like Waltz, is not much help. The war between India and the Sikhs was in no way just. The military actions in which Singh took part were not justified by an established political authority. The Khalistan Commando Force was not authorized to order anything, let alone war. Moreover the conditions of proportionality did not seem to enter his mind. According to the accusations leveled against him, he attacked and killed pretty much at random. Yet in his mind he was part of a situation that made sense and was morally justified. Even when I spoke with him some thirty years after the militant struggle, he showed no signs of remorse for what he did (nor for that matter did he even acknowledge that the charges against him were justified). Singh said that he and his comrades were at war, and, as he put it, "it was what they did."

So my usual sources of scholarly advice were not helpful. But then I found insight in an unusual place: a manual for fighting written by a Prussian soldier in the nineteenth century, Carl von Clausewitz. He is famous for one line from his book, *On War*, the oft-quoted statement "War is the continuation of politics by other means."[4] If that is all that Clausewitz had said, then we could put him in the category of Waltz and other political analysts and move on.

But that isn't all Clausewitz said, and besides, the famous phrase is quoted out of context. If you read the whole book, you will see that to say that war is politics by other means is simply to describe the way war tends to be conducted by states in most cases. It is not war in its essence. For that Clausewitz has coined a much more interesting phrase: "absolute war." This describes how war is imagined more than how it is actually conducted. It is the most extreme form of war, aiming solely to destroy the other side, to absolutely defeat the enemy by whatever means. It is war in the mind before being war on the battlefield.

Clausewitz, who served in various positions with the Prussian and Russian armies, is arguably the world's best theorist of warfare. He was born Carl Philipp Gottfried von Clausewitz in 1780 in Magdeburg, now in Germany, about eighty miles west of Berlin. At that time it was part of Prussia, and Clausewitz's father had been in the Prussian army (though his grandfather was a Lutheran theologian), so Clausewitz also joined the Prussian military, beginning at the young age of twelve. He advanced through the ranks to become a major general, but because of his scholarly nature he was deemed unsuited for most command positions; usually he was assigned instead to administrative posts, though he often served as an advisor on military strategy. He was on staff during several operations, including the Prussian army's incursion into France at the time of the French Revolution, and the Prussian involvement in the Napoleonic War. His best-known work, *On War,* is a bulky manuscript of over four hundred pages that he was still revising at the time of his death. It was published posthumously by his wife. Much of it concerns strategy and how to conduct military operations. But the opening chapters are about theory, about what war essentially is.

It is clear to me that Clausewitz is as puzzled about the idea of war as I am. Having observed war closely, he finds it striking that people can so quickly doff all semblance of civil order and think of themselves as within a sphere of reality where killing other people with impunity makes rational sense. How does one describe the essence of this inverted world-view? Clausewitz came up with the term "absolute war." It is central to his thought and lies behind everything he says about war; it is the perception of reality that undergirds and morally justifies all military action.

As he continued to edit the manuscript, Clausewitz increasingly excised the term "absolute war," preferring the phrase "ideal war," the ultimate idea behind war. For Clausewitz, all war has at its core a common theme: the application of violence to impose one's will on someone or something. This is a winner-take-all combat pitting one brute strength against another. Clausewitz calls this core element of absolute or ideal war *Zweikampf,* "two-sided war," sometimes translated into English as "a duel" because it implies that there can be no compromise and one side must emerge victorious. Other translations of *Zweikampf* use the image of a wrestling match, and in my mind I visualize two Sumo wrestlers grunting with exertion while attempting to shove each other out of the ring.

This kind of absolute or ideal war holds "the foremost place" in Clausewitz's understanding of the nature of war.[5] Yet he realizes that war in this extreme, pure form virtually never occurs in real life (although he did accuse Napoleon Bonaparte of coming close to perpetrating it). Limitations are placed on war for all sorts of reasons—some moral and social but, most important, political. The conqueror may have to rebuild the area after it is conquered, for example, and refrains from total destruction for that reason. Or the triumphant side might, as the United States did in the first Gulf War, end the fighting even when it is ahead, because the limited objectives of the military engagement have been reached. Then again, one might want to obey rules of warfare such as humane treatment of prisoners to encourage the other side to respect one's own soldiers should they be captured. Clausewitz recognizes that absolute war, this harsh but pure ideal form of war, never exists in a political or historical vacuum.

It is for this reason that Clausewitz can say with confidence that ordinarily "war is the continuation of politics by other means." But it is a mistake to think this is his understanding of war. Quite the opposite. For Clausewitz the purest form of war is *Zweikampf,* the all-or-nothing absolute war. At the same time, because war is almost always shaped by the historical context in which it appears, it is also "politics by other means." These two ways of thinking about war are at the two extremes of a spectrum, and most warfare falls somewhere in between. The wars that we can observe are almost always, in Clausewitz's description, "limited wars." Much of the rest of his book is devoted to the limitations imposed on the strategy, tactics, and goals of these wars. They are the kind of war that states manipulate and about which both Waltz and Niebuhr theorize, war that is an extension of state policy, not war in the mind. But Clausewitz begins his book by stating that the concept on which war is based is *Zweikampf,* absolute war—a way of thinking about the world in binary oppositions wherein there can be no compromise.

So the idea of war and war as an instrument of statecraft are two different things. It is true that politicians seize on this notion of war and try to use it to further state policies. And it is also true that they may attempt to stoke the images of war in order to gain support for military ventures. After all, young men and women ordinarily will sign up for combat only if they think that there is a war worth fighting, one that is accepted as legitimate by their peers and compels them to act. The actual conduct of war shows the difficulty in trying to contain these images of absolute war.

In the Vietnam War the "best and the brightest" of the Kennedy administration, as David Halberstam called them, initially made rational calculations, regarding a limited US military engagement in that part of the world as a sensible political option. But to sell the war to the American people it was presented as a great moral conflict from which there was no easy retreat. Later, when the idea had been accepted and the mentality of war had seized the public imagination and many lives had been lost, one presidential administration after another found itself faced with an intractable problem. The logical assessment now—that the war was not worth the terrible cost in lives—was powerless against the momentum of war. Neither victory nor immediate withdrawal seemed possible. "Peace with honor" was the goal, which meant finding a way to disguise a withdrawal as a victory. Something had happened in those years after the first US military advisors set foot on Vietnamese soil, and it had happened not in Vietnam but in the United States: the idea of war had descended into the public consciousness, a mindset from which there was no easy retreat.

Even in warfare conducted as state policy there are distinctions between ordinary war and conflicts that are extensive in scope, in degree, and in kind. Erich Ludendorff, a general in the German army in World War I, wrote a memoir titled *Total War* (*Der Totale Krieg*). In it he implies that the First World War was different from other wars both because of the scale of the military operations and because it was an all-or-nothing combat that targeted civilian populations as well as military positions.[6] Ludendorff's "total war" became the label for the kind of war that is waged not only against an enemy's combatants but against enemy civilians as well. In the Civil War in the United States civilians were also targeted. Union General William Tecumseh Sherman described it as "hard war." Sherman regarded as enemies not only the soldiers in combat on the battlefield but also civilians who provided those soldiers with food and military supplies.

Total war and hard war come close to Clausewitz's ideal type: the imagined absolute war. If he had witnessed the destruction of whole German cities in the carpet bombing of World War II or the atomic bomb blasts that obliterated Hiroshima and Nagasaki, he might have admitted that they came close to absolute war. If he had observed the destruction of Raqqa in Syria, Mosul in Iraq, and Marawi in the Philippines, in the attempt to liberate them from ISIS, he might have viewed those battles similarly. He might also have seen the way that ISIS and Christian groups such as the White Aryan Resistance have viewed their battles and their easy ability to maim, torture, and kill, and described them as engaged in absolute war. And he might have told Surjit Singh that his Khalistani warfare was near the ideal type. Most important, he might have understood Singh's view of the world and realized that he was not articulating a political strategy but speaking about a way of life, a worldview that was radically different from the ordinary template of civil order in which most of us conduct our affairs.

It seems to me that Clausewitz was speaking about an idea of war that was the product of a distinctive worldview, a war worldview. War, or at least absolute war, is an alternative reality. It provides an alternative way of understanding the essential elements of civic order. It upends our view of ordinary reality and replaces it with a way of thinking that is fundamentally shifted in another direction. It is related to our own reality and yet so radically unlike it. To enter into the mindset of warfare is to walk through Alice's looking glass into a vastly different landscape. In the world of war, everything is upside down. It is a world of chaos rather than law, death instead of life, disorder over order. Yet it is strangely reassuring in that it replaces the common markers of civil order with its own alternative.

War's Alternative Reality

It might seem odd to think that war can provide a view of reality that is comforting and reassuring, but it is precisely the view that is promoted in advertisements for the video game Fortnite. This popular game gives players the opportunity to work in teams to combat a horde of zombies that has taken over the world. At the outset, Fortnite presents a world of chaos where civil order has been turned upside down. Zombies roam freely and threaten the basic civilities of life. What to do?

This is where gamers can take charge. Epic Games, the company behind Fortnite, presents the basic premise of the game in a four-and-a-half-minute online promotional video. The first few moments show a devastated city overrun with revolting zombies. Enter the defensive squad, marching down the center of an empty street. They are a young and gender and racially diverse team of warriors, all in the kind of peak physical condition that only months in the gym can produce, clad in warrior-like outfits with leather straps and shoulder pads. They quickly get to work, thinking of ways to combat the undead horde, creating zombie-proof fortresses, and dispatching legions of the zombies with awesome superweapons. The video shows that Fortnite not only portrays a world gone awry—and more than that, a world in chaos—but one in which valiant fighters can take charge and set things right.

Most of the rest of the video focuses on the features of the game and what the player will achieve by entering the war world of Fortnite. In bold letters (the only words superimposed on the action images), the video proclaims that in this game you can "make discoveries," "make forts," "make weapons," and, perhaps most interesting, "make friends."[7] With snappy narration and dramatic action footage, Fortnite advances the claim that its version of war offers opportunities for creativity, leadership, and community. It allows players to take control of a world gone crazy, to identify the enemies (how can one miss them, they are zombies, for heaven's sake), and to triumph over numerous obstacles placed strategically in their path by the game designers. All of the elements of a secure world—authority, identity, social order, and agency—can be created anew out of the rubble of a zombie-ravaged world. But first the zombies themselves need to be subdued. "All we need is a leader," the video narrator says, "and that's you." What's not to like?

Appeals for recruits for real wars are strikingly similar to the advertising for Fortnite—though without the zombies, of course. The Pentagon has studied these games and provides its own version of participatory war games as recruiting devices. Jihadi groups have also created video games.[8] In one produced by the militant Lebanese movement Hezbollah, players can resist Israeli occupation and practice their sniping skills on Israeli political leaders. The game, called Special Force, has sold tens of thousands of copies since it was released in 2005.[9] The Islamic State also entered the video game business. In addition to the presentation of glorious battle in its glossy online magazine, Dabiq, it created online games in which one could vicariously wage jihad on behalf of the caliphate.[10] The Islamic State's 2015 instructional manual for its Western supporters, "How to Survive in the West," included references to video games as a method of training for those interested in joining the group. According to an investigative article in The Atlantic, an American jihadi who joined the Islamic

State was recruited by another gamer whom he met online through a shared video war game.[11] Other terrorists have received online training through video games as well. Brenton Tarrant, who attacked worshippers at two mosques in Christchurch, New Zealand, in 2019, claimed, "*Fortnite* trained me to be a killer."[12] For would-be soldiers like Tarrant their acts of terrorism gave them the opportunities to engage in real-life games.

Like the imagined wars in online gaming, the real wars of militant movements provide alternative worlds in which participants can deal with the chaos and anomalies of life. In my interviews over the years with activists engaged in these wars, I have been impressed with the consistency with which they affirm that their participation was itself meaningful, regardless of the outcome. "It is the excitement and power of being part of something important" that draws them, Jagrup Singh Sekhon told me, explaining the lure of the Khalistan movement for Surjit Singh and the many hundreds of other young Sikh men who joined the struggle.[13]

Though they engaged in acts of violence that their victims and those who observe them might label terrorism, neither Surjit Singh nor any of the other activists thought of themselves that way. They were soldiers, they told me. Their struggles were acts of war. Mahmud Abouhalima bristled when he heard that the charges against him in the conspiracy to blow up the World Trade Center involved terrorism, which he regarded as a pointless exercise. His explanation gave his response more meaning: "We are soldiers for God."[14]

This view of war as moral struggle gives otherwise ethical people the license to kill with impunity. It explains why persons feel victimized and why they need to take revenge for their perceived oppression. It also provides a large worldview, a template of meaning in which their acts of vengeance make sense and receive moral approval. In the context of war, ordinary people can be impressed into service as soldiers, and great confrontations occur in which noncombatants are considered part of the enemy to be destroyed.

When Sekhon said that the allure of the struggle was a sense of empowerment, I think he touched on something that is critical to warfare. After all, it is a participatory activity. Even those who vicariously cheer on the fighters or provide the supplies are involved in the enormous drama of the war worldview. You do not have to simply endure the chaos and disorder of the world; you can actually do something about it.

One reason why the experience of war can be empowering is that it justifies acts of violence. Ordinarily one thinks of violence as a result of warfare. Confronted with an enemy who will destroy you if you don't attack it first, you have the right to slay it—unless you find some other way of getting out of the predicament. In the famous Chinese manual *The Art of War* by Sun Tzu, the most adept forms of warfare are those in which a clever response to an enemy makes actual violence unnecessary. Still, once war has been declared, violence is acceptable.

But the reverse can also be the case: a desire to be violent can create the need for an image of war to justify it. The many Sunni Arab activists who joined the Islamic State were eager to achieve a sense of power, to hold the reins of leadership in their regions of Syria and Iraq. This meant having the ability to control, having the weapons of power. They were not granted that power by civil authority, but adopting a war worldview in which they were a righteous force could give them moral authority.

Wielding the instruments of violence is in itself empowering; leaders or groups who want their roles as arbiters of violence to be justified might well want an excuse to wield such weapons. Images of war stand ready to provide excuses, and for many they are ready at hand within the repository of cultural symbols of their religious community.

When Abouhalima told me that he was not a terrorist but was simply "defending Islam," he was articulating a position that I have heard from many activists who have been involved in militant movements. I interviewed Ashin Wirathu, the anti-Muslim Buddhist monk, in Myanmar shortly after he was pictured on the cover of *Time* magazine next to the words "The Buddhist Face of Terror."[15]

"Do I look like a terrorist?" Wirathu asked me, grinning cheerfully, as if he expected an immediate and resounding negative response. I wanted to tell him that he looked like most of the terrorists I had interviewed, which is to say totally banal.

Such people see themselves as morally pure: they are simply soldiers in a defensive war against a demonic enemy. Wirathu talked about Burmese Buddhism as being under a life-and-death challenge from the forces of global Islam. He asserted that his followers were justified in defending themselves, by violence if necessary, against what he regarded as an insidious threat.

To think of oneself as a soldier can be empowering, and it can also be thrilling in a dangerous way. The possibility of facing life-and-death situations can be one of the more enticing characteristics of war, especially for young men and women who have a penchant for dangerous activity. ISIS, the Islamic movement that for a time maintained a reign of terror in eastern Syria and western Iraq, promoted an enticingly romantic image of warfare for potential recruits from around the world. Their sophisticated media campaign on the internet portrayed a war to defend Islamic civilization and defeat imagined enemies of Islam. It was like an enormous video game that young men and quite a few women could actually join in real life. The recruitment videos and websites give the impression that joining ISIS would be a great adventure and challenge the young recruits to live up to their abilities. Alas, most of them became cannon fodder, cynically used by ISIS commanders eager to control cadres of young foreigners willing to waste their lives in suicide attacks on military targets. But for a time the volunteers were able to act out an exciting life in an imagined alternative world.

Inventing Enemies

Without enemies there would not be war. Without zombies, for instance, there would be no point to Fortnite. The scenario that the game projects is that the zombies take over the world, then mess it up, and righteous people begin to fight back. It is a scarcely veiled analogy to the Nazi takeover of Europe, or perhaps the Islamophobic vision that many Americans and Europeans have of being overcome by waves of Muslims.

No one would care much about a zombie takeover if zombies were nice. If they simply went about their lives in normal ways, opening up florist shops and serving as greeters at WalMart, we would not object to their fictional existence. And if the National Socialist German Workers' Party, the Nazis, had stuck to their campaign promises of a better economy and national pride, they might not have been greatly admired but they would not have been despised. Once non-Muslims get to know Muslim people as friends and neighbors it is hard to dehumanize them. Our attitudes toward others are shaped by the degree to which we think they will actually threaten our existence. After all, like zombies, it is not so much who the others are but what they can do. Absolute enemies are subhuman, capable of destroying the civil order around them.

This is Surjit Singh's view of the Punjab police. I assume that, like most people, ordinarily he grudgingly accepts the need for a police force. He may have been wary of them when he thought they suspected him of committing some infraction but grateful to them when his house was invaded or he was caught in traffic that required police assistance to get things moving again. But when Singh suggested that the Punjab police were one of the reasons he began to think of the world as being at war, what he meant was a pattern of arrest and torture for what he saw as no reason at all, an abuse of power whereby the normal respect for authority in a civil society was turned on its head.

So the idea of an enemy is relative. It depends on how devastated the world has become, and who is blamed for the devastation. Often it is immediately clear who is responsible. If zombies show up, you know you are in trouble. And in many instances of real warfare the enemies boldly present themselves as martial foes. On December 7, 1941, after a massive air attack on US naval vessels stationed at Pearl Harbor in Hawaii, there was no agonized wondering who might have done such a thing. Every American knew at once that it was the Japanese air force: you could see the insignia painted on the sides of their planes. The very next day the US Congress declared that the country was at war.

But sometimes the enemy is not obvious. At times there is an inchoate sense of discord for which there is no obvious origin. In order to make sense of the situation and to wage war against the source of the problem one has to imagine someone or something capable of filling the role of the evil foe. The idea of war is inconceivable without it; war requires enemies. If we sense that terrible things are happening in the world and need the idea of war to explain it, an enemy has to be created even if there is no convincing evidence that there is one, or that the chosen enemy is in fact at fault. The idea of war is the prerequisite to thinking in terms of enemies, and enemies are essential ingredients of war.

In the case of September 11, 2001, the enemies were to some extent obvious. Within days authorities had identified the individual members of the suicide missions that flew commercial aircraft into the World Trade Center and the Pentagon. But it was not clear exactly who the enemy should be. If the perpetrators were only a small band of disgruntled jihadis coordinated by a ragtag organization in the caves of Afghanistan, they would not be much of an opponent. They might not be sufficient to support the concept of war, certainly not a global war. But because war was in the air, the opponents were imagined to be a much grander force of Islamic militancy, involving the collusion of established political rule, not only in Afghanistan but also in Iraq.

The war on terror cast a wide net that encompassed a varied set of possible opponents, though exactly who the enemy was remained fuzzy. Often commentators in the American media identified the enemy with Islam, and the phrase "radical Islam" came into common usage to denote the collective enemy in the war on terror. It was not at all clear what this meant, and some uses of the term seemed to implicate all of the Muslim world. For this reason, President Barack Obama resisted using the phrase, as did his secretary of state, Hillary Clinton. In the 2016 presidential campaign use of the term became a political issue. Opponents of Obama and Clinton accused them of shying away from taking a hard line against America's enemies by refusing to characterize them by that phrase.[16]

In other cases of social insecurity the enemies have been even less obvious. In the case of the Aum Shinrikyo movement in Japan, which unleashed nerve gas in the Tokyo subway system in an act of imagined war, the mélange of their suspected enemies was quite remarkable. It included the Japanese government and the United States, perhaps understandably given the continued presence of American military installations in Japan. More improbable was the inclusion of Freemasons and Jews. It was thought that Freemasons were trying to bring about Armageddon because, in the words of the leader of the movement, Shoko Asahara, "they think the reign of Christ will not come unless the final war is fought."[17] Jews were seen as enemies because of conspiracy theories alleging them to have designs on global economic and political control. Indeed books on the so-called Jewish threat have been popular in Japan.[18] Added to these foes was a vague, generic enemy, a sort of inchoate force of evil, represented by the Japanese police, the news media, and virtually anyone the movement thought might be opposed to it.

The vagueness about who the enemy is in cases like this calls into question one of our usual assumptions about how war comes about. Common sense might suggest that we go to war because we have enemies to fight, but it is often the other way around: the idea of war comes first. War is what humans need in a situation of deep fear about the loss of social order. In order to make that idea of war convincing, there must be enemies. If enemies do not exist as real threats in life, they have to be invented. One has to imagine that there are enemies—people of a different ethnicity, for instance, or distant political powers—who are more threatening than these people actually are.

Most Americans who witnessed the devastating attacks on 9/11 seemed mystified that their country could be regarded as an enemy, regardless of how irresponsible some of its international policies might have been in the past. But from the point of view of the jihadi activists who were looking for the cause of their problems, America was a hidden source of Middle East misery. Peering at the "far enemy" behind the dictators in Saudi Arabia and Egypt and elsewhere in the Middle East, Osama bin Laden and his colleagues found a clear enemy to target. America fit the bill.

Enemies are essential to war. War makes sense only if we see the world as caught within a conflict between absolute opponents. These enemies represent two ways of maintaining order and control in a chaotic world. One leads to clarity and resolution of the disorder; the other leads to more chaos and destruction—indeed it is the source of that discord. The two sides can never be seen as morally equal. It is necessary to the scenario of warfare that one is seen as good and the other evil. No one engaged in a battle thinks both sides are right—at least at the beginning of a conflict. Later, like the protagonist in *For Whom the Bell Tolls,* the participants may see war itself as the enemy of both sides, but this subtlety is lost on the fervent soldiers at the outset of militant confrontation. For them, war is a matter of good guys versus bad guys, a way of defeating evil and bringing the world justice, freedom, and peace.

I think any useful definition of war has to include this ethical component. Perhaps the most basic way of thinking about war is simply this: the moral absolutism of social conflict. It is moral in that it distinguishes between a side that is right and one that is wrong; it is absolute in that the conflict is envisioned in nonnegotiable extremes; it is social in that it is a shared response by a social group to a life-threatening provocation. By "life-threatening" I mean not only an assault that might threaten a people physically but also an existential threat, something that challenges to the core their whole structure of social meaning. Wirathu, the activist monk in Myanmar, claimed that the Muslims in his country threatened the very existence of their traditional culture. "Burmese Buddhism is in danger of being destroyed forever," he told me, "and that is why we must fight to defend it."[19]

The World of War

To see the world at war is to adopt a special lens on reality. It turns everything upside down. But it also provides an all-encompassing worldview. It identifies the sources of good and evil in the world, explains why things occur, gives moral justification to those who lead the battle against evil, and promises victory in the future. It empowers the powerless and gives agency to those who feel marginalized and discarded. It offers a view of ultimate order and a template of social reality that embraces virtually every aspect of life.

Such a totalizing worldview may descend upon a region gradually, the way it appeared to do for Surjit Singh. But it can also be accepted quite suddenly. It is difficult to hold onto two versions of reality—ordinary civil order and a state of war—at the same time. For this reason, some people have described their acceptance of war in a way that sounds much like religious conversion. "That was the most marvelous experience of my life," explained Richard Butler, describing his first encounter with the Christian Identity theory of war. "The lights started turning on, bang-bang-bang," said Butler, the dean of the Identity movement, to a reporter for the *Los Angeles Times.*[20] "Wow, this is it," Denver Parmenter exclaimed, telling how the movement's ideas about ancient and continuing warfare between the races led to a sudden awareness that revealed "the reason things are going wrong."[21] This grand scenario came to him as an epiphany. Kerry Noble, a member of a militant Christian group called the Covenant, the Sword, and the Arm of the Lord, described the moment he embraced the group's vision of a religious war as an "aha experience."[22] The template of war provided a framework of meaning that enabled him instantly to make sense of the world around him. Noble said it was as if he were viewing the world through the fuzzy lens of a camera that suddenly clicked into focus. Now he knew. He knew what had caused the discomfort in his life, what he could do about it, and how the story would end—victoriously, he thought, because the struggle was in God's hands.

To those who experienced them, these conversions to the war worldview were epiphanies; they suddenly were illumined in an entirely new way and began to see everything in the world differently. They felt they finally understood what was really going on in the world, a knowledge that other people did not have. Abouhalima told me that he now had the "real knowledge" about the hidden forces in the world around us. It was, he confided quietly, a war between good and evil, and the US government was the enemy.[23] Abouhalima told me this with the confident satisfaction that he knew something that most people do not. It gave him a powerful and commanding sense of the world. The nineteen hijackers of the airplanes that brought down the World Trade Center and struck the Pentagon on 9/11 most likely also had an exhilarating sense of secret knowledge and a confidence that their act would change the direction of history.

And it did, in a way. The world has not been the same after 9/11, in part because the attacks triggered another view of war in response, the war on terror. US policymakers and the general public latched onto the notion of war as the appropriate way of understanding 9/11. It was not quite a conversion experience, but it did come as a sudden insight; Americans had been naïve in their view of the world and had not realized the magnitude and power of the enemies that would like to take them down. This was an understanding that vastly exaggerated the threat of global jihad, but the events of 9/11 seemed to make it credible. As President George W. Bush described it, it was a battle between good and evil, a dichotomous struggle about which no one in the world could be neutral. They were either for us or against us.

Bush framed the war on terror as a fight for freedom. Like the jihadi ideology of the perpetrators of the attacks, Bush's image of a war on terror had the effect of clarifying what had happened. It put the cognitive anomaly of an attack on the tallest buildings in New York City into a social context, a scenario of warfare that gave the public confidence in a leadership that could identify the enemy and engage in a battle for righteousness that would ultimately succeed. Like all images of war, it was on one level an imagined battle, linked in this case to real acts of military might, including the invasion and occupation of two Muslim countries. The military incursions were vital, for they provided images of power and control to a public that felt confused and weakened.

Such threats to the fundamental structure of one's existence cause desperate minds to seek to make sense of confusion in ordered, though often extraordinary ways. This is where the idea of warfare comes in, entering as a hopeful epiphany. It provides images of enemies behind the chaos, enemies that can be engaged, conquered, destroyed. It necessarily involves ultimate confrontation because it is about ultimate things. The encounter may lead to death. Yet those who engage in this way of thinking, in this war worldview, are uplifted by the notion that the sense of social order and meaning for which they struggle will be redeemed. In a curious way, then, all images of warfare and their awful encounters with chaos end with a hope for peace.

Notes

1. Kenneth Waltz, *Man, the State, and War: A Theoretical Analysis* (New York: Columbia University Press, 1959).
2. Reinhold Niebuhr, *Why the Christian Church Is Not Pacifist* (London: Student Christian Movement Press, 1940).
3. Reinhold Niebuhr, *Moral Man and Immoral Society* (New York: Scribner's, 1932), 134.

4. Carl von Clausewitz, *On War* (1832), trans. Michael Howard and Peter Paret (Princeton, NJ: Princeton University Press, 1984), 87.

5. Clausewitz, *On War*, 80.

6. Erich Ludendorff, *Der Totale Krieg* (Munich: Ludendorffs Verlag, 1936).

7. Fortnite gameplay trailer, Epic Games, accessed July 24, 2018. https://www.epicgames.com/fortnite/en-US/home.

8. Miron Lakomy, "Let's Play a Video Game: *Jihadi* Propaganda in the World of Electronic Entertainment," *Studies in Conflict and Terrorism Journal*, October 23, 2017, https://www.tandfonline.com/doi/abs/10.1080/1057610X.2017.1385903.

9. Rebecca Armstrong, "Jihad: Play the Game," *The Independent*, August 17, 2005, https://www.independent.co.uk/news/science/jihad-play-the-game-5347294.html.

10. Abdel Bari Atwan, *Islamic State: The Digital Caliphate* (Berkeley: University of California Press, 2015).

11. Seamus Hughes, Alexander Melagrou-Hitchens, and Bennett Clifford, "A New American Leader Rises in ISIS," *The Atlantic*, January 13, 2018.

12. David D. Kirkpatrick, "Massacre Suspect Traveled the World but Lives on the Internet," *New York Times*, March 15, 2019, https://www.nytimes.com/2019/03/15/world/asia/new-zealand-shooting-brenton-tarrant.html?action=click&module=Spotlight&pgtype=Homepage.

13. Author's interview with Jagrup Singh Sekhon, professor and head of the Department of Political Science, Guru Nanak Dev University, Amritsar, Punjab, November 27, 2016.

14. Author's interview with Mahmud Abouhalima, U.S. Federal Penitentiary, Lompoc, California, September 30, 1997.

15. Author's interview with Ashin Wirathu, Mandalay, Myanmar, 2015.

16. Max Fisher, "When a Phrase Takes on a New Meaning: 'Radical Islam' Explained," *New York Times*, June 16, 2016, https://www.nytimes.com/2016/06/17/world/when-a-phrase-takes-on-new-meaning-radical-islam-explained.html.

17. Shoko Asahara, *Disaster Approaches the Land of the Rising Sun: Shoko Asahara's Apocalyptic Predictions*, trans. and ed. Aum Translation Committee (Tokyo: Aum Publishing, Shizuoka Japan, 1995), 281.

18. See, for example, Hirose Takashi and Akama Takashi, *The Structure of Japan and the Jewish Conspiracy* (Tokyo: Tokuma Press, n.d.); Uno Magami, *If You Understand the Jewish Situation, You Can Understand the World Situation* (Tokyo: Tokuma Press, n.d.).

19. Author's interview with Wirathu.

20. Kim Murphy, "Last Stand of an Aging Aryan," *Los Angeles Times*, January 10, 1999, A15.

21. Quoted in *Turning Point*, ABC, October 5, 1995, Journal Graphics Transcript no. 150, 2.

22. Kerry Noble.

23. Author's interview with Mahmud Abouhalima.

3

Religion as Alternative Reality

IN SEPTEMBER 2013 Joel Rosenberg was invited to Kansas to meet with Sam Brownback, the state's governor. The topic of the meeting was not Kansas politics or economics, but the situation in the Middle East. Earlier in the year Rosenberg had met with Governor Rick Perry and Congressman Louis Gohmert of Texas to discuss a similar subject.[1]

Rosenberg might seem an unusual person to consult on questions regarding international politics. He is an Evangelical Christian who has described himself as a Jew who believes in Jesus.[2] He is also a novelist, whose books, including *The Last Jihad,* purport to show how present-day events in the Middle East fulfill biblical prophecy.

In his conversations with American politicians, Rosenberg talked about what was going on in Syria. He darkly predicted that the destruction of Damascus would be the forerunner of the end times, and he pointed to a biblical passage in which the prophet Isaiah foresaw the demise of that city as the first step in the process by which God would raise up Israel in the last struggle of earthly times: "Damascus is about to be removed from being a city, and will become a fallen ruin" (Isaiah 17:1).

Rosenberg is not alone in finding present-day political significance in prophetic readings of the bible. End-time prophecies have become big business in the Evangelical subculture and have had a significant influence on the American political right, especially with respect to Israel. Perhaps no presentation of end-time prophecy, however, has had the impact of the *Left Behind* novels and their spinoff movies and video games. Rosenberg's ideas are a logical extension of the religious worldview reflected in these wildly successful publications.

With a combined sales of over eighty million, the *Left Behind* novels have become one of the most widely read and profitable book series

Why God Needs War and War Needs God. Mark Juergensmeyer, Oxford University Press (2020)
© Oxford University Press. DOI: 10.1093/oso/9780190079178.001.0001

of all time. After the first novel, *Left Behind*, came others with titles such as *Tribulation Force, Glorious Appearing*, and *The Rapture*, all of them published by the Christian publishing firm Tyndale House.[3] Between 1995 and 2007 Tim LaHaye and his coauthor, Jerry Jenkins, completed sixteen novels, almost all of which topped the *New York Times* best-seller list as soon as they were published.

The novels offer an account of a group of people who are left behind when a prophecy in the New Testament Book of Revelation comes true and true believers are "raptured" into heaven before the beginning of the apocalypse. Together they repent of their lack of faith, face the rise of the Antichrist, and endure hideous plagues and other acts of judgment from God, most spectacularly the cataclysmic battle of Armageddon and the triumphant second coming of Christ.

Most readers take the books as the fictions they are. But some see parallels with real-world events. Like Rosenberg, they see similarities between the biblical account of Armageddon, which in the novels takes place in the Middle East, and the ongoing conflicts in Syria and Iraq. Writing on the message board of a chat room called "The Prophecy Club" on the *Left Behind* series' website, a woman shared her forebodings about the Iraq War and the continuing unrest in Israel/Palestine. "I have never had such a bad feeling about a war ever before," she wrote. Her "heaviness of heart" stemmed from the portent of worse to come. She was certain that "we are living in the end times and that this war with Iraq is the precursor war to Armageddon." She concluded with the observation "Never have there been so many signs as now in history."[4]

The *Left Behind* novels are set in a world that most readers will recognize as comfortingly familiar: contemporary suburban America. Yet in the midst of the niceties of ordinary life there are rumblings of something profoundly out of sync. The spiritual sterility of what passes for normal society is increasingly evident. A heartless ideology is gradually imposing itself on the social order. Sensitive people—faithful Christian believers—find themselves marginalized, humiliated, and persecuted in a sea of secularism.

But the Christians have, as it were, the last laugh. An airline pilot who dismisses his wife's Christian beliefs and has his eyes on a flight attendant's shapely figure is startled when certain passengers disappear midflight. Believing Christians, including the pilot's wife, are rescued in the event known as the Rapture. With a whoosh, they are whisked away from worldly reality and transposed into the glorious arena of eternal life.

Nothing remains of their earthly existence but piles of clothing dropped in heaps at the moment when their bodies are transported to the higher regions. They would not be naked in heaven, of course; their modesty would be covered by luminous robes provided in the wondrous world of the Lord.

Meantime on sinful and contentious earth are the secularists who are literally left behind at the glorious moment of the Rapture. But also left behind are a band of half-hearted Christians who now realize the foolishness of their ways. They convert to true Christianity, but must await the time for their own moment of Rapture to come. This produces the dramatic tension for the remainder of the series, as the band of newly converted true Christians struggle to keep their faith through waves of plagues and natural disasters and persecutions—the Tribulations—sent by God to punish the sinful. The band of new Christians, who label themselves the Tribulation Force, have to endure the hardships of the reign of the Antichrist, a heartless secularist who just happens to be the secretary general of the United Nations. He uses his position of influence to concentrate all political and economic power under his control in the new world order and renames the United Nations, calling it the Global Community. He even tries to create a new religion in his own name. But eventually Jesus returns, casts the Antichrist and Satan into eternal fire, and the earth is finally redeemed.

The popularity of the *Left Behind* novels is no mystery. For one thing they are fun to read, full of action and simple in their plot lines, with characters who may be portrayed a bit thinly but are recognizable types. They are a kind of religious science fiction. But there is another reason for their success. They tap into a subculture of Evangelical Protestant Christianity, the only segment of organized religion whose numbers have been growing in the United States. By 2015 it was the largest single religious bloc in the country, with 25 percent of all Americans describing themselves as Evangelical Protestants, considerably more than Catholics or members of mainstream Protestant denominations, who came in second and third, respectively.[5]

People who ascribe to Evangelical beliefs may be found in mainstream Protestant churches, but they are the majority in more fundamentalist congregations. Some of these are associated with the Assemblies of God or other denominational structures, but the largest are independent. Typical of these is the Real Life Ministries in Post Falls, Idaho. Founded in 1998, it grew to a congregation of over eight thousand in twenty years. The pastor, Jim Putnam, preaches an unabashed message of premillennial evangelicalism. In addition to the Sunday congregation, the church reaches out to thousands more around the world through podcasts and internet services that are streamed live.

This premillennial Evangelical Protestant subculture flies under the radar of most Americans. Not until the election of President Donald Trump in 2016 did many Americans realize its political power. Many readers of this book may be startled to learn that the *Left Behind* novels are among the biggest sellers of fiction in recent years. But most Americans do not live in this premillennial Evangelical Protestant world. Many do not know what it is all about.

The word "evangelical" is derived from a Greek word meaning "bringer of good news," not unlike the familiar Old English word *gospel*, which means "good tidings." Evangelical Protestants embrace a range of beliefs, but common to most of them is the idea that a believer must be "born again" in a conversion experience, accept biblical authority and its inerrancy, and believe in the Atonement, the doctrine that Jesus died for one's sins and that belief in him brings eternal salvation.

Beyond these are a variety of other beliefs that some, though not all, Evangelicals embrace. Among them are several that lie behind the *Left Behind* novels—the second coming of Christ, for instance. Taking the last (and most controversial) book in the New Testament, the Book of Revelation, as a guide, it is believed that Christ will return to Earth after a millennium and, after a period of great turmoil, usher in a reign of peace. Though it has already been two millennia since this prophecy was written, Evangelicals who accept it believe that the prophesized millennium is yet to come. There are two different camps, however: postmillennialists think that Christ will come and reign over the Earth for a thousand years before the last judgment; premillennialists believe that momentous events will trigger a thousand years of turmoil that must precede the second coming and last judgment at the end of time.

This tumultuous thousand-year period constitutes the "end times" described in the *Left Behind* novels. It begins, according to some, with the Rapture, an extraordinary event when people suddenly vanish into heaven, leaving piles of clothing behind. Rapture theology was popular among Puritan preachers in the early years of the American colonies. In the nineteenth century it was enriched by the teachings of John Nelson Darby, a British preacher who renounced his ordination in the Anglican Church and went on to establish a new denomination, the Exclusive Brethren. He also developed the premillennial rapture theology that became widespread in the American Evangelicalism of the late nineteenth and twentieth centuries. Its popular revival in recent years is an interesting phenomenon and may be a religious response to the social turmoil occasioned by the increasingly secular, multicultural, and globalized urban society of contemporary America. Extreme times call for extreme religion. The *Left Behind* novels allow the reader to imagine the implications of this creative theology for everyday experience. They vividly bring the hidden world of religious imagination to life.

Religion's Alternative Reality

Is the religion embraced by premillennial Evangelical Protestants and portrayed in the *Left Behind* novels authentic Christianity? Well, that depends on whom you ask. It is certainly on the margins of mainstream Roman Catholic and Protestant theological thinking, but these denominations are declining in membership even as the Evangelicals are on the rise, at least in the United States. In Protestant Christianity there is no pope, no final authority on doctrine or practice, so whether or not something is authentically Christian is a matter of opinion. There is no question, however, that it is a religious point of view, and it tells us much about the religious imagination.

The saga portrayed in the *Left Behind* novels presents in an interesting way the worldview of religion in general. It pictures a world of normal reality that is somehow insufficient. Those who are sensitive to deeper aspects of reality perceive this insufficiency and are attracted to a different way of thinking, a hidden truth. This truth informs them that the material world of ordinary reality is in fundamental conflict with a truer, transcendent order provided by religion. In the *Left Behind* novels, this deeper reality is not just hinted at in scriptural texts and Sunday sermons. It crashes into the mundane world with a vengeance, in the dramatic moment of the Rapture.

The tension between the two realities—the mundane world and the religious world—is what most of the *Left Behind* novels are about. They show that the religious reality is more enduring and reliable than secularism, a superficial lifestyle that is mired in the quest to satisfy crass urges for power, money, and physical pleasure. The mundane reality is not just insufficient to provide meaning and comfort; it is downright evil. The battle between good and evil is presented as a challenge to us, the onlookers, who are forced to make a choice, to join one side or the other.

Like Prince Arjuna hesitating at the fringes of the battle in the Hindu epic the *Mahabharata,* the newly converted Christians in the *Left Behind* novels realize that it is not an option to avoid taking part in the battle. The only questions for them are which side they will be on and how they will wage the fight.

It is an imaginary view of the world, to be sure. In saying that, I do not mean to disparage the beliefs of millions but simply to point out the obvious. The language of religion—any religion, be it Evangelical Protestantism or esoteric Buddhism—is imaginary language. This is a point that some theologians have also made. Dietrich Bonhoeffer was a Protestant theologian who left a position at Union Theological Seminary in New York and returned to his native Germany, where he joined a conspiracy to take down Hitler. He was imprisoned and ultimately executed for his role in that plot. Bonhoeffer saw religious activity as a human invention. In one of his letters from prison, he advocated a "religionless Christianity" free from the theological and structural limitations of the church and open to the idea of the indwelling of the spirit, wherever it might be found.[6] The point is that the ideas, practices, customs—everything we think of as being part of religious belief and activity—are products of the human imagination. Believers may affirm that these imaginary ideas and actions are authentic responses to an experience of transcendence, and this may be so. But religion is imagined, all the same.

For this reason many scholars have questioned whether it is even appropriate to talk about religion as if it were a thing, some essentialized entity that can actually do things on its own. In 1963 Wilfred Cantwell Smith, a Canadian scholar of religious studies who for years was director of Harvard's Center for the Study of World Religions, published an arresting book, *The Meaning and End of Religion.*[7] In it he argued that the term "religion" had no analytic value and he advocated discontinuing its use. For one thing, Smith wrote, similar terms scarcely exist in traditions outside of Christianity. Moreover "religion" is a relatively new term even in English. Smith scoured old manuscripts and could find little use of the term before the seventeenth century.

Smith objected to the notion that religion could do anything apart from human agency. He allowed for the continued use of the term in adjectival form—religious roles, religious organizations, religious beliefs, and the like—but not as a noun, because that indicated that it had some sort of independent existence. He preferred instead the terms "cumulative tradition" to describe the cultural heritage associated with the great religious communities around the world, and "faith" in relationship to individual acts of religious belief and practice. Years later another scholar, Talal Asad, refined and expanded on Smith's way of thinking.[8] Asad argued that the term and the idea of religion was a European construct invented in part as a contrast to the idea of the secular.[9] The history of the interaction between secularism and religion in the West has been traced in a magisterial opus by the Canadian philosopher Charles Taylor.[10]

In part because of this scholarly interrogation of the term "religion," scholars of religious studies are somewhat hesitant to employ it, although Smith himself sometimes used the word despite what he had written. He argued that the label "religious studies" implied that the studies themselves were religious. For the department at Harvard, Smith favored "the Program in the Study of Religion," a phrase that Harvard College has used for its undergraduate program ever since. His point about reifying religion by the use of the term has caught on. "Religious studies" is generally the phrase used to describe the study of religious things without implying that religion is in itself a thing that can be studied.

One scholar who departed from this trend was Robert Bellah, perhaps his generation's leading sociologist of religion. Though once a colleague and admirer of Smith and someone who respected both Taylor and Asad, Bellah asserted that it was possible to talk about religion as something in and of itself. He agreed that religion was a product of the human imagination, and that was precisely what interested him. It was not just a matter of religious this or that, for Bellah. The term signified a different way of looking at the world. Where and how did this perspective arise, and what role has it played in human life?

In search of answers to these questions Bellah embarked on a lengthy scholarly journey. He had retired from teaching at this point, so he had the luxury of taking the whole sweep of history into consideration. I knew Bellah during the years he was working on the resulting book; we had been colleagues at Berkeley when I was the coordinator of the religious studies program there and Bellah was the chair of its advisory committee. Now whenever we met, he could not wait to talk about the new nugget of knowledge he had acquired about ancient India or China or about astrophysical theories regarding early forms of life.

Bellah's project was published as *Religion in Human Evolution* in 2011.[11] It is a huge book, as impressive in its scope as it is rich in detail and insight. He takes the long view, beginning 13.8 billion years ago with the Big Bang and the creation of stars and planets, including our own, and then the emergence of living cells in the primal ooze, and the beginning of animate life forms. He ends the book at the Axial Age, the rise of new modes of conceptual activity in the sixth century BCE, a period of intellectual efflorescence around the world, from the emergence of Greek thought to philosophical developments at the end of the Vedic period in India.

It is in this grand historical narrative that he addresses the question of what religion is and relates it to the development of living species. Early life forms, Bellah suggests, are focused on basic material needs, survival and procreation. But later in the evolutionary process more evolved life forms have the leisure of spare time and can do whatever they want. And what they often do is unstructured or arbitrarily structured activity, doing things for no apparent purpose. They are like schoolchildren finally released from their boring classrooms for a few precious moments of recess. What they do during recess is run around and have fun and explore the world. It is what we call "play."

Following the lead of the Dutch historian Johan Huizinga, Bellah argues that play is the beginning of all forms of culture, including religion.[12] It is the human ability to be creative, to roam and discover. Initially it is primarily an activity. The early forms of religiosity—such as the rituals described in Leviticus and in the Vedas of ancient India—are focused on activity, on what priests do to interact with God or the gods.[13] It is only later, in the Axial Age, that religion becomes more introspective and cerebral; this is when we can describe religion as a product not just of creative activity but of creative thought: the religious imagination.

As an illustration of the process by which activity related to religion becomes conceptualized, Bellah describes the development of the Greek idea of *theoria*. Before Plato, this term referred to a practice in which an emissary of one Greek state would go to another state to observe their religious festivals and come back and report on what they saw. *Theoria* was an account of a different kind of religion. Plato took this concept and applied it to the intellectual adventure of going out to search, not for religious festivals but for truth. The classic example is the analogy of the cave. Plato says that most of us venturing into the cave see shadows cast on the wall and think they are what is truly real. If we turn around, the bright light behind the objects whose shadows we saw would be so intense that most of us would flinch and turn back to the shadows. Only the bold would go in search of the real objects, the truth. These are the *theoria* that Plato admires, the searches for truth. Later Aristotle would refine this further in a way that we all know, in which the idea of theory is related to identification of truthful concepts.[14]

Religion in Bellah's understanding is some thing, or rather some perception. It is an imagined world of being, "a general order of existence," as the anthropologist Clifford Geertz describes it. Bellah goes further, labeling it "religious reality," one of multiple realities that "calls the world of daily life into question."[15] Here Bellah allies himself with a school of sociology associated with the Austrian philosopher Alfred Schütz, who held that reality is socially constructed. The American philosopher William James, who saw cultural forms as constructions of the social imagination, is also an influence.[16] This idea, made popular by the book *The Social Construction of Reality* by Peter Berger and Thomas Luckmann, is that what we perceive as everyday reality is a social construction of what things are and what they mean.[17] A wooden table, to most humans, is a place to put books and plates of food, but to a termite it is a feast. It all depends on your point of view. What Bellah adds to this conversation—aided by the thought of the pioneering French sociologist Émile Durkheim—is the insistence that religious perceptions are also constructions of reality.[18] The table might, for instance, be an altar in a religious reality. These religious realities are among the varied multiple realities that most people navigate every day. These multiple realities can present meanings that are quite different from one another even though they relate to the same thing, just as we and termites see tables differently though the table remains the same.

Thinking about religion as alternative reality gives us a whole new perspective on the *Left Behind* novels and the religious worldview behind them. Like the characters in the novels, the true believers in premillennialist Evangelical Protestantism think there are deeper realities beneath the superficial appearances of everyday life. They might not have seen the Rapture, but they certainly think it's possible that one day they will be flying in an airplane or walking down the street and, whoosh, people will start disappearing, leaving little piles of clothing behind. They are likely to be suspicious of political leadership and efforts to forge a new world order, knowing—as they believe they do—that the Antichrist can adopt just such a posture. They are convinced that eventually there will be a last judgment and the faithful will be redeemed, while unbelievers and sinners will pay for their transgressions and burn in eternal flames.

It is a remarkable view of the world, but not that dissimilar to many other, less extreme religious realities. They may not contain an antichrist or a rapture or a last judgment, but the fundamental dichotomy between the ordinary world and the alternative reality of religion is there, even if the religious reality in question is simply a subtle awareness of a deeper stratum of meaning in the world. It may just be the certainty that there is an ultimate reality, as the Protestant theologian Paul Tillich described it. For many, however, and an increasingly large number of Evangelical Protestants, it is a vibrant and startling reality that could break into the normal world at any moment. Behold, the rapture may be at hand.

To accept the alternative reality of religion is to peer through the looking glass and see that there is a Wonderland behind the ordinary world, only a few steps away. Like Wonderland it both mirrors ordinary reality and alters it. It provides an alternative source of authority—clergy and scripture, in the case of Evangelical Protestantism—that can challenge or supplant the laws and authority of the state. It can give a sense of identity that is more sure than the national identity associated with being a citizen of a given country. The religious identity is often transnational, and loyalties to it can challenge state loyalties. The alternative reality of religion can also provide community, a kinship with fellow faithful that can be more binding than any allegiance to a political party or national society. The alternative reality of religion is not a passive gift; one must do something to find it. One must believe and follow its commandments.

Responding to Life's Disorder

For those who accept it, the Wonderland of religion is comforting simply because it exists. It provides a way of thinking about the world—an alternative vision of reality—that takes the disturbing uncertainties of life, the anomalies, the dangers, and the nagging sense of chaos, and gives them meaning. It locates disorder within a triumphant pattern of order. It does this especially effectively in thinking about the most difficult moment of chaos in one's personal life: one's death.

In Japan, where the religious traditions of Shinto and Buddhism are intertwined, it is the Buddhist strand that is prominent at the time of a person's death. The funeral is held several days after death and involves a wake, then the funeral proper with a Buddhist priest reading from the sutras, cremation, and burial. At the time of the funeral the Buddhist priest assigns a new name to the deceased, the Buddha name that will prevent the soul from returning and help to speed the departed into eternity. The elaborateness of the name will depend in part on the fee the family is willing to pay. Often they will come up with a sizable sum because the purpose of the name, the prayers and sutras, and all of the ritual is to help maneuver the dead person's soul through the tortuous journey of the afterlife and elevate it in the heavenly abode.

Hindu death rituals have the same purpose, though in Hinduism the idea is not to help a soul achieve a higher status in heaven but to help it be born into a more auspicious body in the karmic cycle of life and rebirth. As in Japanese Buddhism, the priestly rituals at a Hindu funeral pyre are for the benefit of the dead, intended in a way to cheat death of its victim by providing a religious conduit to a life in the hereafter.

In Christianity the religious encounter with death occurs at the very heart of Christian worship. The central moment is the Eucharist, also called Holy Communion or the Lord's Supper. Protestants may celebrate it only on special occasions, such as Easter. In the Roman Catholic, Orthodox, and Anglican tradition the Eucharist is enacted in most services of worship. In Roman Catholic churches the Eucharist must be present for a service to be considered Holy Mass; otherwise the service is called "Lessons and Prayers," or "Morning Prayers," or some other term according to the type of ritual and time of day in which it occurs. What makes the Eucharist special is that it is a sacrament, thought to be an occasion for an act of God.

This divine action comes in the blessing, or consecration, of the "elements"—wine and bread. Each worshipper eats a tiny portion of blessed bread and sips a few drops of consecrated wine (or grape juice in many Protestant denominations, water in Mormon services).

"Take, eat; this is the body of Christ, broken for you," the celebrant usually says during the distribution of the bread. "Take, drink; this is the blood of Christ, shed for you, drink this in remembrance of Him," the celebrant repeats in offering the wine. Later, as the worshippers prepare to leave, the celebrant will often say these closing words of blessing: "Go in peace, and the peace of the Lord be with you."

What has happened in this ritual moment? On one level it is simply a sacred snack. On another level it is divine cannibalism. It is a reenactment of a hideous event, the torture and death of Jesus, after which, it may appear, the faithful pounce on the body and consume it. The Eucharistic table is the church's altar. It is a table, an apt symbol of the meal that the congregants consume together. But it is also the vestige of a much older religious artifact: the chopping block on which blood sacrifices were offered, after which the dead animals were consumed.

The Eucharist reenacts what in Christian memory is a sacrificial death. It recalls the Jewish seder meal, which was the last meal of Jesus Christ, who as a good Jew was celebrating the Jewish season of Passover shortly before his death. But the "body" and "blood" that the bread and wine represent point to the sacrifice of Jesus himself. According to most theological interpretations, Christ offered himself as a sacrifice on behalf of all of us, sinners who deserve punishment and eternal death. By offering himself as a sacrifice he atones for our shortcomings and enables us to secure eternal life. Hence, as Saint Paul famously wrote, "Christ died for our sins" (1 Cor. 15:3). It thus makes sense that the crucifixion is the central Christian moment and its primary symbol. It recalls what was fundamentally a sacrificial act.

This central idea of sacrifice unites Christianity with virtually every other religious tradition on the planet. All have images of sacrifice. In one case the same sacrificial story is shared by three different religious traditions, a story involving the biblical patriarch Abraham. Judaism, Christianity, and Islam all venerate the occasion described in Genesis 22:1–19 when God tests Abraham by calling him up the mountain and commanding him to sacrifice his own son (Isaac in the Christian and Jewish versions, and Ishmael in the Muslim version). But at the last minute, before the knife is applied to the boy's neck, a ram (a goat in the Muslim version) appears in a thicket to be sacrificed instead. This story is behind one of the most sacred days in the Muslim calendar, Eid al Adha, "Festival of Sacrifice." On that day throughout the Muslim world, goats are brought to mosques to be slaughtered and to commemorate the miracle in which a similar animal was offered up as a substitute when the patriarch Abraham was commanded by God to sacrifice his son.

Martyrdom is also a kind of self-sacrifice. Calendars in Sikh homes are adorned with pictures of warfare and the sacrifices that Sikh leaders have made in fighting for the faith, including vivid images of the beheading of one of the founding ten gurus, Guru Tegh Bahadur. In Shi'a Islam, the martyrdom of the founder, Hussain, is seen by the faithful as a sacrifice as well.

Sacrifice—particularly blood sacrifice, the offering of an animal or even a human—is one of the earliest forms of religious activity and is found in every ancient religious tradition. The Vedic Agnicayana, some three thousand years old, is probably the most ancient such ritual, and is still performed today in southern India. It involves the construction of an elaborate altar for what some claim was originally a human sacrifice.[19] Human sacrifice was said to be at the center of elaborate rituals in the ancient Aztec Empire in South America, in which conquered soldiers became the sacrificial victims. They were treated royally in preparation for the sacrifice, then set upon with knives, their still-beating hearts ripped from their chests and offered to Huitzilopochtli and other gods, eventually to be eaten by the faithful. Their faces were skinned to make ritual masks.

In contemporary forms of religious expression, no humans are harmed in sacrificial events, and few animals for that matter. Rather, sacrifice is usually presented in a symbolic or metaphorical way. But the historical texts of the traditions portray a bloodier past. One cannot read the Hebrew Bible, sacred to Jews and the first books of the Old Testament in the Christian Bible, without being overwhelmed with the precision of the instructions for how sacrificial rites were to be carried out.

There is a good deal of specificity about the sort of animal required for the sacrifice. In the Book of Numbers, for example, it has to be a "red heifer without defect," on which "there is no blemish, and upon which a yoke has never come" (Numbers 19:2). The priest is required to take the heifer outside the camp and slaughter it, and then with his finger take some of the blood and sprinkle it at the front of the main tent of the camp seven times. Then the priest presides over the burning of the heifer, along with perfumes and sweet-smelling wood. Afterward the priest has to wash his clothes and bathe since he is ritually unclean. The ashes of the burned heifer will be retained for special occasions, when some will be mixed with water and sprinkled on the faithful for the removal of sin (Numbers 19:10).

Clearly something is going on here that is more significant than simply burning a cow. This highly specific ritual process is a way of integrating death and life, impurity and purity, sin and redemption. It is a curious procedure and it raises the basic question of why such gory acts of sacrifice are so central to religion. That question has preoccupied scholars for over a century, from Émile Durkheim and Sigmund Freud to contemporary theorists such as Maurice Bloch, René Girard, Walter Burkert, and Eli Sagan.[20] The theories are diverse and sometimes contradictory, but there are some common themes. These theories focus on sacrifice because it is ubiquitous to religion and can be traced in most cases to antiquity, but for two other reasons as well. One is that the scholars sense that something about this rite is fundamental to the religious imagination. If one can make sense of it, one can understand religion itself. Another common observation is the obvious one: that sacrifice is an attempt to understand and overcome life's most disturbing anomaly, death.

Almost every religious tradition deals in some way with death, and most have some promise of existence beyond it. The Mahayana Buddhist idea of the Pure Land, the Christian idea of heaven, and Hindu cycles of reincarnation all offer ways of overcoming the fear of what humans know to be fact, that eventually they will die. Ernest Becker has called this religion's "denial of death."[21] I agree with Becker, but what strikes me as particularly interesting is the way religion incorporates death into life by domesticating symbols of violence—the sword and the cross, for examples. These remind the faithful not only of death but of religion's ability to tame and overcome the violence associated with it.

Images of violence, rituals of death, and rites of sacrifice are all a part of the armament of religion for dealing with life's deepest anomaly: human mortality. They permeate all aspects of religiosity and are at the heart of the large structures of religious activity and meaning that make each religious tradition distinctive. For example, the distribution of the sacrificial elements of the Eucharist takes place within a ritual designed to magnify the differences between the sacred and mundane levels of existence and to highlight the tension between them. The dramatic moment of ritualized sacrifice in Christianity occurs in the context of struggle and despair. The inadequacies of the human condition—its weakness and confusion—are overcome in the recognition of a divine intervention that tips the balance in favor of humanity and rescues the fallen. Thus the sacrifice becomes a metaphor for salvation, and salvation the resolution of an eternal conflict— the apotheosis of a grand and timeless war.

Religion and War: Competing Realities

As we saw in chapter 2, war provides an attractive alternative view of reality in a time of social discord. The war worldview begins with a nagging sense of discomfort, the feeling that somehow the social order is gravely out of place. Phenomena like political oppression or events like the attack on the World Trade Center can trigger this experience of disquiet. War becomes a way of explaining things, of making sense out of the senselessness of reality. It is a way of dealing with disturbing aspects of life and offers a way out of them.

The alternative reality of religion is strikingly similar to the alternative reality of war. The worldview of war provides a way of making sense of social chaos, explaining a world gone awry. In a curious way, the religious worldview does much the same thing. In the case of religion, however, it is not just a social anomaly that is experienced but an intensely personal one: confrontation with the reality of mortality and one's own impending death. Religion, like war, can take the fear of discord and not only mask it but provide a template for action by which one can overcome the forces that lead to the discord, and thus banish the fear.

The religious worldview is like the war worldview in other ways as well. The promotional video for Fortnite highlighted the elements of the appeal of its imagined war; these are precisely some of the same things that are attractive about the imagined world of religion. Both offer alternative forms of authority that parallel the established leadership of a political regime, an identity that gives a unique sense of being and purpose, and membership in a community—an army or religious fellowship—that binds its members together more closely than any civil society can do. Both war and religion are calls for action, commitment, and participation. One can surely exist in both the world of the alternative reality—war or religion—and in everyday life. As Bellah has said, we have the ability to live with multiple realities that overlap in our daily lives. But for many true believers in either war or religion, the alternative reality will ultimately challenge and supplant the ordinary order.

Religion and war seem to operate in the human imagination in similar ways. The French scholar Roger Caillois observed that war "possesses to a significant degree the character of the sacred."[22] Religion—by which I mean the religious imagination of an alternative reality—does in a symbolic way what war does. It begins with a state of discord and incompleteness. For most worshippers, the recitation of prayers is an invocation of their own limitations, their sinfulness, and most of all their mortality. To be reminded of the human condition is, after all, to be apprised of its inevitable end. Religious images of sacrifice revel in this reality and expose it in what might appear to be a brutal way. In the cathedrals of Central American cities, one frequently finds a life-size figure of Jesus in what appears to be a glass coffin, as if he had been brought straight from the cross. The bloody wounds from his crucifixion are still glowing in vivid red. Yet to the faithful these are positive images, since the end of the sacrificial ritual—and the end of the Passion narrative of the crucifixion and resurrection of Christ—is like the end of war. It is the transformation of death into life.

These aspects of religion support the idea of an unseen source of power and meaning in the world, a source that is usually imagined to be on a transcendent plane of reality. This is where God comes in, a term that combines the ideas of ultimate power and certitude in a way that is vivid and sometimes portrayed anthropomorphically. The idea of warfare need not contain the notion of God enabling it, but there is likewise a sense of the inevitability of ultimate victory for those who adopt its perspective, the sense that their own sacrifices on the battlefield will not be in vain.

Both war and religion present an alternate order of existential tension and moral contest that encompass any apparent anomalies in life, such as bombing attacks or the persistence of sinful mortality. The main difference is that war offers a mundane form of alternative reality, a different way of understanding the configuration of social order, whereas religion provides a vision of a transcendent order of reality. God rules.

For those who have adopted a perspective of the world at war, war wins. What is comforting about both of these ways of thinking is that those who accept them are convinced of ultimate victory. Those who adopt a religious perspective imagine God to be ruling on their side; those who believe in war are assured that they will conquer. Both religion and war provide alternative visions of power and meaning in the world that ennoble humans both as individuals and as communities and exalt them beyond their messy, confused, and mundane worlds and, by allowing them to stare into the face of death, ultimately to conquer it as well.

Notes

1. Tim Murphy, "Oh Magog! Why End-Time Buffs Are Freaking Out about Syria," *Mother Jones*, September 4, 2013.

2. Joel Rosenberg, "My Spiritual Journey," Joel Rosenberg Website, accessed July 22, 2018, http://www.joelrosenberg.com/my-spiritual-journey/.

3. Tim LaHaye and Jerry B. Jenkins, *Left Behind: A Novel of the Earth's Last Days* (Carol Stream, IL: Tyndale House, 1995).

4. Quoted in Melani McAlister, "An Empire of Their Own," *The Nation*, September 22, 2003.

5. Pew Research Center, "America's Changing Religious Landscape," May 12, 2015, http://www.pewforum.org/2015/05/12/chapter-1-the-changing-religious-composition-of-the-u-s/#the-shifting-composition-of-american-protestantism, chapter 1, "The Changing Religious Composition of the U.S."

6. Dietrich Bonhoeffer, *Letters and Papers from Prison*, ed. Eberhard Bethge (New York: Simon and Schuster Touchstone Books, 1997), originally published as *Widerstand und Ergebung: Briefe und Aufzeichnungen aus der Haft* (Munich: Christian Kaiser Verlag, 1970).

7. Wilfred Cantwell Smith, *The Meaning and End of Religion: A New Approach* (New York: Charles Scribner's Sons, 1962).

8. Talal Asad, "Reading a Modern Classic: Wilfred Cantwell Smith's *The Meaning and End of Religion*," *History of Religions* 40 (2001): 205–222.

9. Talal Asad, *Genealogies of Religion: Discipline and Reasons of Power in Christianity and Islam* (Baltimore, MD: Johns Hopkins University Press, 1993).

10. Charles Taylor, *A Secular Age* (Cambridge, MA: Harvard University Press, 2007).

11. Robert Bellah, *Religion in Human Evolution: From the Paleolithic to the Axial Age* (Cambridge, MA: Harvard University Press, 2011).

12. Johan Huizinga, *Homo Ludens: A Study of the Play-Element in Culture* (1944; London: Routledge, 1949).

13. The philosopher and Indologist Frits Staal has analyzed ritual in ancient India and emerged with a theoretical conclusion that ritual in general is simply patterned random activity and has no inherent meaning at all. J. Frits Staal, "The Meaninglessness of Ritual," *Numen* 26.1 (June 1979): 2–22.

14. Bellah, *Religion in Human Evolution*, 577.

15. Bellah, *Religion in Human Evolution*, 5.

16. Alfred Schütz, *Phenomenology of the Social World*, trans. George Walsh (Evanston, IL: Northwestern University Press, 1967); William James, *The Varieties of Religious Experience* (1902; New York: Penguin Classics, 1985).

17. Peter Berger and Thomas Luckmann, *The Social Construction of Reality: A Treatise in the Sociology of Knowledge* (New York: Penguin Random House, 1966).

18. Émile Durkheim, *The Elementary Forms of the Religious Life*, trans. Karen Fields (1912; New York: Free Press, 1995).

19. J. Frits Staal, *Agni: The Vedic Ritual of the Fire Altar* (Berkeley, CA: Asian Humanities Press, 1983).

20. Maurice Bloch, *Prey into Hunter* (Cambridge, UK: Cambridge University Press, 1992); René Girard, *Violence and the Sacred*, trans. Patrick Gregory (Baltimore, MD: Johns Hopkins University Press, 1977); René Girard, *The Scapegoat*, trans. Yvonne Freccero (Baltimore, MD: Johns Hopkins University Press, 1986); Walter Burkert, *Homo Necans: The Anthropology of Ancient Greek Sacrificial Ritual and Myth*, trans. Peter Bing (Berkeley: University of California Press, 1972); Walter Burkhert, René Girard, and Jonathan Z. Smith, *Violent Origins: Ritual Killing and Cultural Formation*, ed. Robert G. Hamerton-Kelly (Stanford, CA: Stanford University Press, 1987); Eli Sagan, *The Lust to Annihilate: A Psychoanalytic Study of Violence in Ancient Greek Culture* (New York: Psychohistory Press, 1972); Eli Sagan, *Cannibalism: Human Aggression and Cultural Form* (New York: Psychohistory Press, 1974).

21. Ernest Becker, *The Denial of Death* (New York: Simon and Schuster, 1973).

22. Roger Caillois, *Bellone ou la Pente de la Guerre* (Paris: Flammarion, 2012), 151. This English translation of the quote from the book is in Arnaud Blin, *War and Religion: Europe and the Mediterranean from the First through the Twenty-First Century* (Oakland: University of California Press, 2019).

4

The Marriage of War and Religion

AMONG THE VOLUNTEERS who heeded the call of the Islamic State to
come to Syria and Iraq and join the army of the caliphate were identical
twin brothers from the Ruhr region of western Germany. Unlike most of
the ISIS recruits from abroad, Mark and Kevin Knop had not been raised
Muslim in an immigrant community.

The blond, blue-eyed lads were born in 1989 in the town of Castrop-
Rauxel near the city of Dortmund, where the prevailing religion was Roman
Catholic. Their parents were devoted to them. Their father was a police of-
ficer. They appeared to have had a conventional childhood, an upbringing
dedicated to school and sports. According to an internet-accessible curric-
ulum vitae obtained by the German magazine *Der Spiegel*, Kevin was the ad-
venturesome one of the pair, in high school venturing abroad to California
on a year-long student exchange program.[1] In 2009, after graduating from
high school and before beginning college, Kevin again spent another year
abroad, this time in Istanbul. There he apparently became interested in
Islam. When he returned, he entered Ruhr University in Bochum, where
he studied law, excelling in a program focused on the legal aspects of energy and mining law. At the same time he began regularly attending a
mosque for prayers led by Hasan Celenk, a colleague of the radical Muslim
cleric, Abu Walaa, in the northern city of Hildesheim, who is said to have
recruited a number of Germans for service to ISIS.[2]

In the meantime, in 2010 Kevin's brother, Mark, had signed up for
a four-year stint with the German military and served a tour of duty in
Afghanistan. He and Kevin kept in touch, and Kevin apparently persuaded
Mark to take Islam seriously. In 2012, according to *Der Spiegel*, during a
break from his military obligations, Mark underwent conversion to Islam
in a mosque in his hometown, presumably with his brother at his side.[3]

Why God Needs War and War Needs God. Mark Juergensmeyer, Oxford University Press (2020)
© Oxford University Press. DOI: 10.1093/oso/9780190079178.001.0001

The German military authorities got wind of Mark's increasing radicalism, and in 2013 he was declared a security risk and discharged from the army.

In August 2014 the twins told their mother that they were going to Turkey on vacation. They were in fact going to Turkey, but not on vacation. They slipped over the border into Syria and joined the forces of the Islamic State. Their letters home assured their parents that they were well and were filled with heartfelt expressions of commitment to their new faith and to the cause of the Islamic State.

The twins had been with ISIS in Syria and Iraq for only a few months when Mark was assigned to a strategic mission. Early in 2015 ISIS commanders were seeking to cut off the supply line between Baghdad and the city of Fallujah. The critical connection in the supply line was a military base. In a carefully planned assault, in May 2015, ISIS fighters distracted the Iraqi army defenders of the post and were able to open the main gates.[4] Mark, now dubbed Abu Mus'ab al-Almani, was at the wheel of an armored military vehicle loaded with seven tons of explosives. He barreled through the opened gates into the heart of the military complex and blew up the vehicle, instantly destroying the base and obliterating everyone around the vehicle, including himself. Weeks later Kevin too conducted a suicide mission. The ISIS online propaganda magazine *Dabiq* proclaimed them both to be *shahid*, martyrs, and devoted an article to praising their bravery and their commitment to the faith.

I confess a certain fascination with this case, in part because my own family emigrated from this region of Germany to the United States over a century ago, and the Jürgensmeier family farm still exists in a village not too far from Dortmund. I have had students with Middle Eastern backgrounds who have been targets of ISIS recruitment—fortunately unsuccessful. But this case hits even closer to home: Kevin and Mark could have been my distant cousins.

For most Germans, as for most Americans, the question is *Why?* Why would these average young men with reasonably successful careers have abandoned it all to seek momentary glory as soldiers for the Islamic State, a mission they must have known would quite likely end the way it did, with their tragic deaths?

Does Religion Lead to War?

One answer to why the German twins pursued a path that led to war and death has to do with religion. The motivations of supporters of ISIS are diverse, however. There is no one answer to why people joined the movement.

In some cases it clearly was for political power and social acceptance. The Sunni mullah whom I met in a Baghdad mosque shortly after the US invasion was quite clear about why his people took part in the resistance: they were fighting for ethnic pride and empowerment. Later, when ISIS emerged as the representative of Sunni claims to political power, it was understandable that many Sunni Arabs would join. As a social group, they had been left out of the power circles of both Iraq and Syria; Shi'a rather than Sunni Muslims were charge. In the ethnoreligious politics of those two countries Sunnis were made to feel like second-class citizens. The Islamic State gave them a land of their own. Whether or not they were interested in the religious aspects of the movement, ISIS employed and empowered Sunni Arabs in what amounted to a Sunnistan of ISIS-controlled territory.

In other cases, especially the thousands of young men and women—perhaps as many as thirty thousand of them—who flocked to the region from around the world, the motives were probably more complicated. When ISIS sent out the call through its glossy media and sophisticated internet social networks, some who felt marginalized in their country of residence may have been attracted to battle in order to find social acceptance. The young Algerians in Brussels, for instance, were members of an immigrant community that was not fully welcome in Belgium. Others may have come for the excitement, as soldiers of fortune seeking the thrill of being part of a glorious battle, whatever it was for. Yet others may have had religious motivations.

Religion could have been the appeal for the German twins. In the brief sketch of their life history in the German media, the progression seems clear: first they became interested in Islam, then they became converts to a fundamentalist form of the faith, and this led them to join ISIS, where they became soldiers in the battlefields of Iraq and Syria and were promptly killed. In the narrative supplied in newspaper and magazine articles, the implication is fairly predictable: their interest in religion led to their participation in war.

Behind this narrative is the assumption that religion has the capacity to drive people to war. That is an interesting assumption. To test it empirically, one would have to isolate religious factors from all other possible motivations and see if religion in fact was the driving force. I know of no study that has done that, at least successfully, so we are left with anecdotal accounts that are subject to the observer's prejudices. The question remains: How likely is it that religion by itself leads to violence?

In *The Way of the Strangers: Encounters with the Islamic State*, the journalist Graeme Wood explores the role of religion in the background of ISIS activists.[5] The book is based on interviews with supporters of the radical Salafi Islamic school on which the ISIS ideology relies heavily. Though Wood never says it, the focus on religious ideas alone may give readers the impression that this is what leads to violence. This impression is buttressed by the way the book is structured. It starts with the Salafi views expressed by an Egyptian tailor and goes on to more radical versions of that vision. A discussion of Salafi fundamentalism proceeds to Salafi thinking about jihad. The discussion about fighting the forces of evil leads in turn to the role of religious ideas in real acts of violence. For many readers, the implication will be clear: radical religious ideas lead to violence. Thinking about the world in terms of confrontation leads to real conflicts.

Curiously, though, none of the men Wood interviewed for his book actually went to the front lines; none literally picked up a sword or donned a suicide belt in defense of his version of the faith. Wood tells us that most Salafi Muslims are nonviolent; even those who espouse a jihadi worldview seldom act on it in violent ways, including those whom Wood interviewed. Some of those who do act violently were described in an earlier article by Wood in the *New Republic* that identified three types of people who fight for ISIS: "psychopaths," "true believers," and "Sunni pragmatists." Presumably the religious motivations are characteristic of only the "true believers"—but it is still not clear why some "true believers" go to Syria and Iraq to fight and others stay home and cheer them on.

I conducted my own interviews among refugees in Iraq who had fled from ISIS-controlled areas and had lived in Mosul and Ramadi and other areas of Iraq under ISIS control. I asked them whether they thought the fighters' motivations were political or religious. Most agreed that their motives were political, although one thought for a moment and ventured that the motivations may have been partly religious, but that it was "a strange religion."[6] It was not his kind of Islam. When I interviewed actual ISIS fighters in prison in 2019 after the end of the conflict, I found that their motives were mixed: some proclaimed that the idea of an Islamic caliphate was the main attraction; others focused on the mistreatment of their Sunni Arab communities in Iraq and Syria as the reason for their anger and the attraction of a Sunni-led ISIS regime.

So it remains unclear whether or to what extent religion is the key to understanding the choice to participate in the ISIS movement. Though I do not discount the possibility of a role for religion, it seems to me that it would have to be examined on a case-by-case basis. I don't think it's fair to assume that, because religion is in the background, it is what has propelled people into violence.

But this is precisely the assumption that is popular with a certain segment of the general public in Europe and the US. The idea that religion leads to violence has become almost a mantra. Leading the charge are several aggressive atheists, such as Richard Dawkins and Sam Harris, who contend that the very nature of religion leads to violence. "Religion causes war because it generates certainty," Dawkins is frequently quoted as saying, and that recent acts of terrorism were motivated by religion because "only religious faith is [a] strong enough force to motivate such utter madness in otherwise sane and decent people."[7] Harris, a neuroscientist, chimes in with what seems to him obvious, that "religion is the most prolific source of violence in our history."[8]

On the other side are the sympathizers of religion, who feel called upon to defend it against what they contend are spurious claims. In a well-researched book, *Fields of Blood,* Karen Armstrong surveys the history of religion's relationship to violent actions. She analyzes specific cases in depth and concludes that these are political confrontations in which religious language is used to justify and support a conflict that is based on social confrontation and the acquisition of power. Armstrong ends with this observation: "The problem lies not in the multifaceted activity that we call 'religion' but in the violence embedded in our human nature and the nature of the state."[9]

I tend to agree with Armstrong more than with Dawkins in this debate, but I'm not really comfortable with either side. What is missing from both is an exploration of the actual role that religious language and ideas play in real situations involving violence. Is religion simply part of the social identity of people who are fighting for their community? Are leaders of the battle clerics who rely on religious authority for their leadership? Do they use the flag of religion to urge the faithful into war? Or is it the case that scripture inspires people to slay the infidels, any infidels who may be at hand? One would have to examine each instance to determine the role of religious ideas or images or scriptures or leadership or social identity in each individual act of violence.

Behind all of these questions about how particular aspects of religion may be related to violence is a more fundamental question: Is religion an entity that can cause anything at all, let alone violence?

This is indeed a basic question, and it touches philosophic depths. Karl Marx asserted that social conditions give rise to ideas, rather than ideas producing social change. In so doing, Marx claimed that he "stood Hegel on his head."[10] Mainstream social science is hardly Marxist, but it owes something to him and other early sociologists. In general, ideology is thought to emerge from social relations and not the other way around. It is partly for this reason that religion is often ignored in the social sciences.

As a social scientist myself, I tend to accept this materialist perspective, and my instinct is to question whether ideas of any sort play a major role in motivating social actions. When presented with a religious or other ideological worldview, I usually want to know who holds these ideas and why and what is in it for them. I don't absolutely deny that ideas, including religious ideas, can play an important role, but my instinct is to see these ideas in social, economic, and political contexts rather than as disembodied entities that can influence things on their own.

Still, as I have said, I agree with Robert Bellah that religion is something. Maybe it is not an entity, but it is a collective perception, a worldview, an alternative reality. As an alternative reality it provides a template of meaning for people who have embraced that perception. The end-times worldview of premillennialist Evangelical Christians provides believers with the conviction that behind ordinary reality is the contestation of great forces of good and evil, and that at any moment the world as we know it may be interrupted by dramatic, transformative events, like the Rapture and the tribulations described in the Book of Revelation. But does that belief in an alternative religious reality lead in some cases to violence? It is an interesting question. Certainly another construct of alternative reality—war—almost by definition leads to violence. So we might ask how the alternative reality of religion is related to the alternative reality of war.

War and religion play roles in human imagination that are so similar they could easily reinforce one another. Both provide alternative perceptions of order, ways of seeing the world that absorb anomalies and explain why chaos and disorder exist; they explain and ultimately contain and control these untidy and dangerous aspects of life. War's alternative reality is a this-worldly version, and religion offers a transcendent vision, but they function so similarly that the two are often found in tandem. War frequently utilizes religion, and religion often incorporates images of war.

Still, war and religion are perceptions of reality—alternative realities. They are not entities capable of action on their own. Neither war nor religion is an agent that can do things by itself. When I say "war leads to violence," I mean that war's perception of a world locked in absolute moral conflict can provide justifications for acts of violence within that sphere of reference. The degree to which religion is involved in the justification of violence depends on the relation of religion to war.

There are several ways to think about this relationship. When we think of war embracing religion, we usually mean those occasions when religious images, ideas, and organizations are employed to buttress notions of war. When we say that religion embraces war, we usually mean those moments when images of war are crafted to buttress ideas about religion. The relationship between religion and war depends on which perception of reality is the dominant one.

When War Embraces Religion

Let us return to the problem of Kevin and Mark, the German twins who became jihadis and martyrs. Why did they do it? What was the appeal? Were they in it for the religion or for the war?

At one point in Wood's book, he reports a conversation with an Algerian supporter of the Islamic State who defended the movement against the charge that it violated the principles of Islam. Responding to Wood's assertion that ISIS had too much "killing, slavery, amputation," the man said that he understood, but he explained in simple terms why it all made sense: "This is a war."[11]

The implication is that in this case, war trumped religion. He may have seen ISIS ideology as the fulfillment of Islamic prophecy. He may have agreed that ordinarily religion is a moderating force regarding the use of violence. Most Muslims, including most Muslims of the extremist Salafi variety, are nonviolent. But when it came to the necessities of acquiring power and administering control, the Islamic State had to do what it had to do. This meant following the dictates of war.

This is something that anyone can understand, from marginalized Sunni Arabs in Iraq to disaffected immigrant youth in Brussels who have been raised on battle-saturated video games. ISIS has proclaimed that a war is going on, a big war, and it has opened its doors to anyone who wishes to join the adventure. The language of religion helps, to be sure. Even the most ignorant fighters are reassured when they are told that this view of war is authenticated by scripture and tradition and is legitimate, although they might not know or even want to know the specifics. For them the fighting is the point: to be engaged in a great battle that will give their life meaning.

Thomas Hegghammer, a Norwegian author who has followed ISIS perhaps more closely than any other scholar, has written extensively about "jihadi culture." He argues that the allure of the movement does not mainly lie in its ideas but in its total worldview, a view of a world at war, a war sustained by a diverse remnant of the faithful who have created their own community and culture.[12] Their worldview is everything. Their community and culture are all-encompassing. But these are not solely social and political entities, and they are not secular. Religious ideas do play an important and formative role and have helped to frame their disturbing and destructive worldview.

In virtually every war—especially a great war, a war of a magnitude that threatens the very existence of a people and their culture—God is enlisted on both sides. A videotape smuggled out of Afghanistan soon after 9/11 shows Osama bin Laden using his hands to depict the moment when the two airplanes struck the Twin Towers. It might have looked to many like boasting. But the Al-Qaeda leader quickly corrected that impression, saying that this was a great act of God, and its success was due to God's graciousness.

At that very moment flags were waving throughout the United States in solidarity against the perpetrators of the act that brought down the towers. "God Bless America" was everywhere on bumper stickers, and that patriotic anthem rang out throughout the country. Soon God appeared to be backing the war on terror, as the fervor of religiosity was fused with the fever of war, first in Afghanistan and then in Iraq. On the eve of the attack on Fallujah in 2004, one American commander[13] rallied his troops with the clear message that their assault was directed by God. It was not true that they were fighting an unseen enemy; he knew who the enemy was and his name was Satan. The overwhelming majority of military chaplains in all branches of the U.S. armed forces are Evangelical Protestants for whom the language of religious war comes quite easily.

Warfare often unites nationalism with religious purpose—fighting for "God and country." In time of warfare few leaders can resist the temptation to claim God for their side. Fewer still would emulate the humility that Abraham Lincoln purportedly displayed when asked whether God was on the Union side in the Civil War. Lincoln was quoted as saying that he did not know which side God was on, but he certainly hoped that he himself was on God's side.

Religion is an attractive ally in time of warfare because it provides a host of benefits. Religious language frames the contest in absolute terms and clarifies the all-or-nothing nature of the struggle. It demonizes opponents and valorizes the leaders of one's own side. Religion provides moral justification for killing and eternal rewards for martyrs. Religious institutions offer a ready-made network for recruitment and provide the blessings of moral authorities. Religious images can personalize a political struggle, showing that the foe is responsible for one's own hardships and that political success is tied to spiritual redemption that is personally experienced. In this sense, war can be seen as part of religion's essentially transformative promise of salvation.

The ideas that witches exist, or Jews are a problem, or all Muslims are terrorists are inventions of a shared perception. All of these claims belong to alternative worldviews of war in which evil enemies needed to be invented in order for that worldview to be viable. Someone has to be the scapegoat. This is where religion provides conceptual support for a war worldview.

Since I have defined war as the moral absolutism of social conflict, one might well ask whether all wars are to some extent religious wars. I think the answer is, in part, yes. Because all wars involve the conviction that enemies are evil and good must prevail, ideas of religion are often in the background. As we have seen, it is easy for sacred language and images to be enlisted for a military cause. Most wars are thought (or at least said) to be conducted for a high moral purpose, and often this means proclaiming them to be blessed by God. There is a sliding scale between worldly war and religious war, between military actions that represent rational calculations for the sake of civil order and those that are seen as manifestations of a sacred struggle. Those who think about how we might live in a world without war must deal with the religious dimensions of the construct— the images of spiritual war that may be lurking behind military operations and their public supporters—as well as with the worldly causes for which a war might be waged.

When Religion Embraces War

The German twins Kevin and Mark may well have been lured into the jihadi struggle by the glamor of war. Mark had already served a tour of duty in Afghanistan and perhaps was eager to enter into a conflict that he saw as more meaningful and in which his role was more direct. It probably helped that the jihad was justified by his newfound religion.

Then again, religion might have been his primary motivation and war simply a burdensome commitment that came with the package. Ordinarily, however, when images of warfare appear within religious worldviews those images are sanitized and bent toward the purposes of religion. They are meant to validate the religious worldview by means of analogies and symbols. For that reason, religious ideas themselves seldom lead to actual war.

This may seem a surprising claim—that when religious language speaks of war it does not often lead to a real fighting war. After all, images of warfare are ubiquitous in religion. Wherever you turn in the history and mythology of religious traditions you bump into war, whether the great conflicts of the Hindu epics the *Ramayana* and *Mahabharata*; the wars between Buddhist and Tamil kings in the Sri Lankan chronicles; the grand adventures of Japanese and Chinese Buddhist warriors; the biblical accounts of warfare in the books of Exodus, Numbers, Deuteronomy, and 1 Samuel; or the triumphant wars of Islamic tradition that can be traced back to the military exploits of the Prophet. In the case of Christianity, as depicted in the *Left Behind* novels, we find the ultimate war before the last judgment. It would seem that warfare is an image that religion can scarcely do without.

It is true that the idea of warfare has become internalized in most religious traditions. At the very beginning of the Bible, in the book of Genesis, the creation of the world is presented as the triumph of order over chaos. This narrative is thought to have its origins in earlier Babylonian mythology about the war against chaos, *Chaoskampf*, as it is known to textual scholars. In the ancient Babylonian epic the *Enuma Elish*, the world is created by conquering the chaos monster, who is split in half, separating the earth from the heavens, exactly the way it is described in the first book of Genesis (Genesis 1:6–8).

The war between good and evil within each person is a frequent theme in most religious traditions. It is what jihad means to most pious Muslims: the battle for purity that rages within each person's heart. When I was a teenager growing up in the Protestant Bible Belt of the American rural Midwest, itinerant preachers would come to revival meetings and preach about the battle of the spirit that we young people were faced with, urging us to gird our loins and side with the good. I recall one preacher dressed in camouflage-patterned fatigues proclaiming that there was a real war going on—a real war between good and evil. It was necessary for each of us to make a decision right there and then, a decision for Christ that we would join the struggle and tip the battle against Satan and the forces of evil.

Our Protestant hymns were full of battle. We were exhorted to march "onward, Christian soldiers," as if we were "going on to war." Other hymns challenged us to "stand up, stand up for Jesus" as "soldiers of the cross," to fight "the good fight," and struggle "manfully onward" to subdue the enemy, identified in this case as "dark passions," and as teenagers we knew what that meant. Harriet Crabtree, a scholar of popular Protestantism, surveyed the common images in what she called the "popular theologies" projected in the hymns, tracts, and sermons of modern Protestant Christianity. She found that the "model of warfare" was one of the most enduring and pervasive.[14] The Protestant writer Arthur Wallis argues in his book *Into Battle* that "Christian living *is* war." For Wallis this is not "a metaphor or a figure of speech" but a "literal fact"; however, "the sphere, the weapons, and the foe" are spiritual rather than material.[15]

The Indic traditions of Hinduism, Buddhism, and Sikhism present a panoply of battle images. We have discussed the fierce battles that consume much of the narrative of the two great Hindu epics, the *Mahabharata* and the *Ramayana*. The Theravada Buddhist text, the *Mahavamsa*, chronicles great battles between Sinhalese Buddhist and Tamil kings. The calendar art of popular Sikh culture vividly portrays the bloody encounters with the Moghuls including the martyrdom of two of the founding gurus in the Sikh lineage, Guru Arjan and Guru Tegh Bahadur. Though he was beheaded in a military encounter with the Mogul army, some calendar art portrays another Sikh hero, Baba Deep Singh, as still fighting manfully on, sword in one hand, and his severed head in the other.

What should we make of these tales of bloody battles and gory images? Sikh theologians and writers, like their Christian counterparts, explain such stories about warfare allegorically. They point to the war between belief and unbelief that rages in each person's soul. Interpreters of Jewish and Islamic culture have transformed the martial images in their traditions in a similar way, for example as seen among those Muslim writers who speak of the true jihad as the one within each person's soul. The chroniclers of the Hebrew Bible have interpreted acts of war as God's vengeance, undertaken by the divine so that humans will not have to fight.

Thus violent images have been given religious meaning and been domesticated by them. Although presented visually and in stories as terribly real, these violent acts have been sanitized; they have been stripped of their horror by being invested with religious meaning. They have been justified because they are part of a religious template that is even larger than myth and history; they have become elements of a ritual scenario in which people can experience vicariously the drama of transcendent war.

In most religious portrayals of warfare, religion rises above the messiness of life, its disorder and its end in death. When religious cultures portray warfare as acknowledged and ultimately controlled, they offer an almost cosmological reenactment of the primacy of order over chaos. When the creators of the stained-glass windows of the great European cathedrals portrayed Christ as king, emerging from his grave like a general victorious in battle, they were asserting something fundamental about Christianity (and every other religious tradition): religion affirms the primacy of order over disorder, of life over death. To make this point, however, violence and other forms of disorder must be vividly portrayed and ultimately conquered.

The irony of these bloody images is that faith has always longed for peace. But in order to portray a state of harmony convincingly, religion has to show disharmony and portray its ability to contain it. Religion has dealt with violence not only because it is unruly and has to be tamed but because religion, as the ultimate statement of meaningfulness, always has to assert the primacy of meaning in the face of chaos.

It is also true, however, that people within all religious traditions have engaged in real violence in ways that incorporate religious symbols and images. Followers of the Shiv Sena in India—the "army of Lord Shiva"—have appropriated the image of Shiva's sword in savage attacks on Muslims in the city of Ahmadabad. Christians have entered battle with the hope that God was on their side, and Muslims have waged what they have characterized as holy wars.

Critics of religion like Dawkins and Harris rush in, pointing to these examples as proof of how religion leads to violence. They have a point, of course, since religion has undeniably been an element in many instances of violence in recent years as well as throughout history. But it returns us to the question of causation: Is religion using war in these instances, or is war using religion? It is true, as Dawkins says, that the language of religion is absolutist, sometimes dogmatic, but so are many other totalizing ideologies. Is there anything about religion that by itself conduces to violence?

One of the most peculiar notions—oddly popular in the general literature—is that violent images in scripture inspire the faithful to act in a similar way in real life. The idea, I take it, is that people may be sitting in their comfortable living-room chair reading scripture, and when they come to the passages about war they will suddenly be so fired up that they will run out of the house, sword in hand, looking for infidels to slay on the spot.

I suppose such a scenario is possible, but it's not likely. There are millions of Muslims in Asia—where most of the world's Muslims live—who read the Qur'an faithfully and do not seem to be propelled toward violence. Violence associated with Islam seems to occur mostly in areas of the world with severe social and political tensions. Moreover there are even more millions of Christians and Jews reading scriptures that are even bloodier than the Qur'an, and few of them seem to be motivated to violence simply on the weight of textual examples. It seems unlikely that biblical texts or theological positions in themselves lead anyone into warfare and violence.

Dawkins is a biologist and Harris is a neuroscientist. Neither is a scholar of religion. No scholar of religion would say what they say without careful qualification and evidence to support his or her position.

Hector Avalos is one genuine scholar of religion who does argue that religion itself conduces to violence, but his approach is quite different from that of Dawkins and Harris. Rather than firing a broadside against the history of religion in general, Avalos takes seriously the notion of religion as alternative reality, as a worldview. His argument is that the idea of religion involves a scarce resource, spiritual truth, and that competition over this asset is what may lead to violence.[16] It is an interesting argument, though not one that has gained much acceptance. In any event it is quite different from the simplistic idea that reading violent scriptures leads to violent actions.

Most religious studies scholars would agree that the role of warfare in religious language and tradition is ordinarily metaphorical. When religion is overtly a part of warfare, as in the case of the Shiv Sena in India or some Christian militias in the United States, we usually find that war is using religion. When war embraces religion, war is exalted and religion is servile to its purposes. But when religion embraces war, religion is exalted and war is the symbolic servant, and a domestic servant at that. War is thus neutered by religion. Only rarely is religion involved in warfare in a more direct way.

When War and Religion Are Fused: Cosmic War

When people like the German twins convert to a new religious belief, they are usually not motivated to go to war. But the German twins were ready for war, it seemed, as soon as they completed their religious conversion—or perhaps because of it. What made their situation different? Where they attracted to war or to religion? Or could they have been attracted to both?

One of my students told a story that sheds light on how ISIS recruits new converts to the cause. Ayman (not his real name) was raised in southern California. His family was originally Palestinian, and he wanted to become more proficient in Arabic, so he took the opportunity of a summer language immersion program in Amman, Jordan. There he had a revealing and frightening encounter.

Ayman had befriended several Jordanians his own age. One afternoon they asked him if he wanted to join them on an outing. "Sure," he said, eager to get to know the local culture better, to practice his Arabic, and to bond in fellowship with his new friends.

With two of his friends, he piled into a car driven by someone he had not previously met. Another newcomer was there as well. They began driving toward the mountains on a route that seemed purposely circuitous. Before long Ayman was confused about the direction from which they had come and equally uncertain about where they were going. The car stopped to accept another stranger, and Ayman began to become suspicious about the purpose of the outing.

The afternoon light was fading by the time they reached their destination, a hilltop surrounded by a grove of trees. They left the car and spread out in a circle in a clearing, enjoying the twilight calm, the breeze, and the distant mountain views. The driver began talking, and the others were clearly deferential to him and respectful of his message. He wanted Ayman to know how special he was, he said, in associating with more than one culture. But he should not forget where his people came from or their suffering.

The message became increasingly personal. Others in the circle began to add to the driver's comments. They talked about Ayman's obligations to his community and to himself, the need to seek a more meaningful existence, to be a part of something more important than oneself. They also talked about a coming apocalyptic moment in world history. There would be a confrontation between the forces of good and evil, and he could be a part of that momentous struggle.

At this point Ayman was beginning to get the picture, and it was a picture he didn't like. He thanked them for their friendship and their insights and asked them to return him to his room. At first they wanted to talk with him further, but seeing that he was not ready to be receptive, they relented and told him to think about what they had said and they would discuss it again.

There was no second meeting, however, and Ayman made sure to keep a respectful distance from the friends who had brought him to the hilltop. I asked him whether he thought they were trying to recruit him into their view of religion or into war. He seemed puzzled by the question, and after a moment's hesitation corrected me, saying, "They were trying to recruit me into ISIS."

He had a point. For this recruiting party, as perhaps for the German twins, ISIS was both religion and war. We have already considered the phenomena of war embracing religion and of religion embracing war. ISIS offered an intriguing third option, in which it appears that the religion is war and the war is the religion.

In an interesting book, *ISIS Apocalypse,* William McCants makes the argument that the worldview of ISIS is a vision of sacred confrontation that is both religion and war.[17] Probing the theology of the ISIS leadership, McCants shows that their ideas are rooted in a marginal Islamic notion of extreme prophecy. Not altogether unlike premillennial Evangelical Protestants, ISIS leaders imagined that history is moving toward a cataclysmic confrontation between the forces of good and evil that will result in a whole new era of righteous order. The main difference between the Christian end-time beliefs and the ISIS apocalypse is that the ISIS leaders have thought that before the savior comes—the Mahdi in prophetic Muslim apocalyptic thinking—a new caliphate has to be established by means of real battles conducted by righteous Muslim soldiers. In other words, their religious worldview is a world of war.

Not all supporters of ISIS bought into this apocalyptic scenario, at least not as enthusiastically as many of the leaders. My interviews with Sunni Arabs in Iraq, including former ISIS fighters and refugees from ISIS-held territories, suggest that most of the ISIS foot soldiers from the region were motivated by a desire for Sunni Arab empowerment. And many of the foreigners who have flocked to the region have been drawn by the allure of war, any war. They craved the excitement and thrill of a slightly sketchy, dangerous encounter, without any apparent real knowledge of or even interest in the theology behind the war worldview.

There is no question, however, that the apocalyptic image of righteous religious war is what appealed to some of the former ISIS fighters I interviewed and most of the movement's leaders. And it is what has animated them. In *The Way of the Strangers*, Wood says that for many of the followers of ISIS, "this war is the main event in human history—not a skirmish decades away from the end." He quotes the Swedish scholar Magnus Ranstorp, a former director of the Centre for the Study of Terrorism at St. Andrews University in Scotland, as saying that for those who embrace this vision of religious war, joining the Islamic State is "better than getting tickets to the World Cup," since it's like being able to "play in the championship and score a goal."[18]

This is an instance where religion and war are fused. This fusion creates a powerful construct of human imagination that elsewhere I have called "cosmic war."[19] It refers to the idea of a radical divine intervention in human history, an existential battle between religion and irreligion, good and evil, order and chaos. It is a remarkable combination of the concept of religion and the idea of war that is often expressed in real war and not just in its literary and legendary representations. When it takes on a life of its own and is not contained within the symbolic language of religion, it can present a whole new kind of alternative reality that is both religious and bellicose.

Even when one embraces the idea of cosmic war, however, real war does not necessarily follow. We have seen that some Christians have taken the idea of apocalyptic war from the book of Revelation, as portrayed in the *Left Behind* novels, and have imagined it as cosmic war without actually fighting anyone because of it. They do believe, however, that current events are evidence that it is coming to pass. The cataclysm described in Revelation 16 includes a battle, but it also involves a series of acts of nature presumably triggered by God: "flashes of lightning, loud noises, peals of thunder, and a great earthquake such as had never been since men were on the earth" (Revelation 16:18). Islands would vanish and mountains would be leveled (16:20). At the culmination of the conflict the old world would be swept away and "a new heaven and a new earth" would be established (21:1). A new holy city, a new Jerusalem would rise up and God would dwell with the inhabitants. "Behold," the book says, "I make all things new" (21:5). Some Christian activists saw the global war on terror as signaling that apocalyptic moment described in Revelation. It was cosmic war, God's war, a war predicted in the Bible.

Millenarian movements have erupted more than once in Christian history, often in response to dire social and economic conditions. Norman Cohn has chronicled some such movements that arose in Europe's late Middle Ages, including the Anabaptists, the Ranters, and the movement led by the theocratic king John of Leiden, who took over the city of Münster in 1534.[20] Other religious traditions also contain apocalyptic visions similar to the second coming that is awaited in Christianity. In Judaism it is a first coming, in that the Messiah, David, has not yet appeared for the first time. It is his coming that is anticipated by Messianic Jewish Zionists in Israel who want to take over the West Bank to prepare the biblical land of Israel for his return. Rabbi Meir Kahane described this as "catastrophic Messianism": the Messiah will arrive after a period of real earthly conflict.[21] In Hinduism there is the expectation that Kalki, a future avatar of Vishnu, will return in the golden age of Satyayug. According to the German religious studies scholar Perry Schmidt-Leukel, this Hindu idea is picked up by Buddhists in the eleventh century, with the Kalki figure reimagined as a redemptive Bodhisattva.[22] This idea in turn influenced Islam. So the notion of a savior figure at the end of days is not unique in religious history. But it is not necessarily the occasion for earthly war.

Most believers in the end times, and most readers of the *Left Behind* novels, are not violent. They are willing to accept that this cosmic war, if it ever occurs in the real world in real time, will come in the future, most likely after their own lifetime. Or if they expect it to happen sooner it will be like an act of God, a sudden event over which they have no control. It is not something that they will actively engage in by plotting attacks on secularists or acts of terror against secular authorities.

Some end-time activists, however, do see themselves as part of the struggle now. They think that the end times are already upon us and the time has come for them to take up arms, to defend the righteous and sow fear in the hearts of the secular enemy. In Christian compounds in Arizona and Idaho, they have created survivalist communities where they are hunkered down, heavily armed and self-sufficient, preparing to do battle with the secular authorities if necessary. At Ruby Ridge, Idaho, in 1992 one white separatist and end-times believer, Randy Weaver, engaged in an eleven-day standoff and shootout with the FBI that resulted in the deaths of a federal marshal, Weaver's wife, and one of his sons.

Some Islamic activists also see their struggle as part of a cosmic war. They may, like the leaders of the Islamic State, imagine that they are entering into an apocalyptic struggle at the end of history, or they may accept that the cosmic war will ultimately be waged on a transcendent plane, and the earthly skirmishes of the present are but the harbingers of a more glorious confrontation to come. The ninth section of the Qur'an urges the faithful to stand up in righteous defense against "people who have violated their oaths and intended to expel the Messenger" and those who "attack you first" (Surah 9:13). The historical context is the seventh century CE, when the fledgling Muslim community was struggling to survive in a hostile environment on the Arabian Peninsula. However, some Muslims take this Qur'anic passage as a clue that a cosmic war is even now being waged in transcendent time, and the faithful are being called to struggle against those who would try to destroy them and their religion. Like the battles in the New Testament Book of Revelation and the Hebrew Bible, it is ultimately not a human battle but God's war: "Fight against them so that Allah will punish them by your hands and disgrace them and give you victory over them and heal the breasts of a believing people" (Surah 9:14).

Curiously this idea of ultimate apocalyptic war recently surfaced in far-away Japan. Borrowing the name of the battlefield in the final confrontation described in Revelation 16, the Buddhist Aum Shinrikyo leader, Shoko Asahara, described his own vision of Armageddon. This apocalypse, he predicted, would rival World War II in its destructiveness. Most Japanese would take this to mean something even more horrific than the nuclear annihilation that was visited on the cities of Hiroshima and Nagasaki. Asahara prophesied that such nuclear devastation would be multiplied and compounded with biological and chemical nerve gas attacks. The movement's imagined enemies were a paranoid cornucopia of political powers and social groups, from the Japanese government and the US military to the Freemasons. The Aum Shinrikyo imagined itself to be the lone defender of all that was good in civilization. Their terrorist attack in 1995 was meant to illustrate this imagined view of religion and war, and by illustrating it bring it into reality. If the sarin gas they unleashed in the Tokyo subways had been a purer strain, tens or even hundreds of thousands of Japanese commuters could have been killed. In the event, twelve innocent subway riders perished in an agonizing way, and six thousand were injured. Asahara was tried and convicted for his part in this incident of terrorism, and in 2018 he was finally executed along with six of his co-conspirators.

The ideas of spiritual battle found in scripture are employed by activists in such disparate movements as the Aum Shinrikyo, the Christian right, and militant Islam. They are shadows of the war images that exist within the worldviews of many religious traditions on a symbolic level. These images are played out in the legends and stories of most traditions on an epic scale. Ordinarily images of cosmic war are confined to myth and symbol, but when they are superimposed on real-world social and political confrontations those who believe in them can be swept up into a grand scenario of warfare. Conflicts over territory and political control are elevated to the high proscenium of sacred drama. Such images of cosmic war are metajustifications for religious violence. They not only explain why religious violence happens—why religious persons feel victimized by violence and why they need to take revenge for this violence—but also furnish a comprehensive worldview, a template of meaning in which religious violence makes sense. Righteous people are pressed into service as soldiers and great confrontations occur in which noncombatants are killed. But ultimately the righteous will prevail, for cosmic war is, after all, God's war. And God cannot lose.

The idea of cosmic war has much in common with Clausewitz's notion of the ideal type of war, war in its purest form—"absolute war." It is the image of a great confrontation between two sides locked in an all-or-nothing struggle, a confrontation so grand and complete that it is almost always confined to the imagination and to representations in myth and legend. Forms of this apocalyptic narrative are found in popular culture—in the *Left Behind* novels, for example, and in such video games as Fortnite and Counter-Strike. What makes the idea of cosmic war different from absolute war, however, is the nature of the struggle. Cosmic war is a contest not just between two earthly combatants but between essential forces of reality. It has an existential valence; it is a fight between good and evil, right and wrong, order versus chaos.

I have not used the term "holy war" to describe this union of religion and war for several reasons. One is that holy war is usually associated with Islamic ideas, and the notion of cosmic war exists in virtually every religious tradition; it is not solely Muslim. Moreover distinctions are sometimes made by scholars and activists between holy war and divine war; one is war undertaken on behalf of God, and the other is war imagined to be carried out by God. Holy war is not quite cosmic war since it is somewhat limited by moral and social constraints, in the way that Clausewitz speaks of the political and social limitations placed on absolute war; "just war" is even more explicitly limited by the moral rules that it places on military engagement. Cosmic war, however, has no such limitations. It is absolute war on an existential level.

When cosmic war bursts from its confinement in myth and legend and is transposed onto real earthly confrontations—such as the territorial raids of the Islamic State—it can change the nature of the conflict. For one thing it expands the horizons of the confrontation. It expands them spatially in that cosmic war is not confined to one region or location on earth but rather is a manifestation of a global conflict between forces of good and forces of evil. It is also expansive in a temporal sense, for cosmic war can endure beyond one's lifetime and still ultimately end in victory.

When I challenged Dr. Abdul Aziz Rantisi, the political head of Hamas, regarding the efficacy of Hamas's methods—especially suicide attacks—against the powerful Israeli army, he acknowledged that it would be difficult for Hamas to triumph in his own lifetime, or even in his children's lifetime.[23] But in his children's children's lifetime, Rantisi said, his face brightening, "we may succeed." He declared that they could not possibly lose since this was not their own battle but "God's war." In a cosmic war, defeat in a skirmish or the deaths of warriors are temporary setbacks in a struggle that could persist for decades, even eons, because it is in God's time. But because it is "God's war," as Rantisi put it, the ultimate outcome has been preordained, and the virtuous side will prevail.

In a real-life conflict the notion of cosmic war is useful in recruiting warriors. It promises them personal redemption and heavenly rewards. Cosmic war is a social construct that is usually shared by a group of people who collectively are defensive or disturbed about the world. The idea of cosmic war gives clarity to their confusion and direction to their anger. It is also intensely personal. It challenges individuals to accept this world-view in a conversion experience and provides personal rewards, including spiritual transformation and redemption. The "Last Instructions" manual found in the car of one of the 9/11 hijackers after his death specified rites of purification to be performed before the final mission. This was a sign that perishing in the suicide attack would make the hijackers martyrs and redeem them in the afterlife.

Cosmic war can promise other heavenly rewards, although the importance of this has perhaps been exaggerated. Much is made of a promise in the Qur'an that all pious Muslim men will receive sensual rewards in heaven, consorting with virgins. Some stories about the Prophet (in the *hadith*) that were written after the revelations of the Qur'an specify that the number of virgins will be seventy-two and that they will have almond-shaped eyes and large breasts. However, the videotaped last testaments of young Palestinian men who have volunteered for acts of suicide terrorism do not dwell on these heavenly rewards, but rather on how they will be remembered in the community's history and that their act will make something positive of their lives. They also expect to be exalted in heaven as part of their spiritual rewards.

Others have joined the jihadi mission hoping for earthly rewards. Their spiritual quest might be fused with hopes for earthly power, privilege, and acceptance in the jihadi community. Many have seen in ISIS a glimmer of hope for their sense of self-worth, the hope that the caliphate will transform not only Syria and Iraq but their own lives and put to rights a world askew. A teenage follower of the ISIS cyber network living in Canada, reached online by the Canadian scholar Amarnath Amarasingam, reported that his parents were taking away his computer to prevent him from being in contact with the ISIS network. They wouldn't succeed, he said, as he had other ways to get online. He needed this connection, he explained, because he felt more true to himself online with the jihadi network than in any other aspect of his teenage Canadian existence. He added, "I never felt like I've belonged anywhere until I met the brothers and sisters online."[24]

Was this what animated the German twins Kevin and Mark when they joined the movement? Were they seeking meaning in life and a profound sense of mission and community, or were they also seeking transcendent rewards? We will never know which of the promises of cosmic war appealed to them or why they so willingly gave their lives to the Islamic State's cause. We do not know whether they sought religious fulfillment, the thrill of war, or both in the fusion of religion and war I have called cosmic war. My guess is that it was some combination of these, that cosmic war was likely in their imagination. This is the template of religious war that the ISIS propaganda arm has displayed in its online magazine *Dabiq* and is echoed in chatter among the global jihadi cyber community on social media. If Kevin and Mark entered into that world, it was both thrilling and redemptive, engaging and ennobling. They likely fell into its black hole, a dark alternative world of cosmic war, from which they would not return.

Notes

1. Jorg Diehl and Roman Lehberger, "Islamischer Staat is Wirbt mit Terror Zwillingen aus Deutschland," *Spiegel Online*, May 27, 2015, http://www.spiegel.de/politik/ausland/islamischer-staat-is-wirbt-mit-terror-zwillingen-

aus-deutschland-a-1035688.html. The twins' last names were usually not published by the German press out of respect for the privacy of their surviving family members.

2. "'ISIS Ambassador to Germany' on Trial for Recruiting Jihadists," *Local De*, September 26, 2017 and Georg Heil, "The Berlin Attack and the 'Abu Walaa' Islamic State Recruitment Network," February, 2017, 10:2, *Combatting Terrorism Center Sentinel*, https://ctc.usma.edu/the-berlin-attack-and-the-abu-walaa-islamic-state-recruitment-network/.

3. Diehl and Lehberger, "Islamischer Staat."

4. "The Capture of the 4th Regimental Base in Wilayat Shamal, Baghdad," *Dabiq*, no. 9 , 29, May 2015.

5. Graeme Wood, *The Way of the Strangers: Encounters with the Islamic State* (New York: Random House, 2017).

6. Author's interview with refugees from ISIS near Mosul, February 11, 2017.

7. Richard Dawkins, *The God Delusion* (New York: Mariner Books, 2008), 343.

8. Sam Harris, *The End of Faith: Religion, Terror, and the Future of Reason* (New York: Norton, 2005), 26.

9. Karen Armstrong, *Fields of Blood: Religion and the History of Violence* (New York: Knopf, 2014), 412.

10. Karl Marx, *Das Capital*, 102–103.

11. Wood, *The Way of the Strangers*, 248.

12. Thomas Hegghammer, *Jihadi Culture: The Art and Social Practices of Militant Islamicists* (Cambridge, UK: Cambridge University Press, 2017).

13. Mike Marquesee, "A Name That Lives in Infamy," *The Guardian Website*, November 10, 2005, https://www.theguardian.com/world/2005/nov/10/usa.iraq.

14. Harriet Crabtree, *The Christian Life: Traditional Metaphors and Contemporary Theologies* (Minneapolis, MN: Fortress Press, Harvard Dissertations in Religion, 1991).

15. Arthur Wallis, *Into Battle: A Manual of Christian Life* (New York: Harper, 1973).

16. Hector Avalos, *Fighting Words: The Origins of Religious Violence* (New York: Prometheus Books, 2005).

17. William McCants, *The ISIS Apocalypse: The History, Strategy, and Doomsday Vision of the Islamic State* (New York: St. Martin's Press, 2015).

18. Wood, *The Way of the Strangers*, 264.

19. Mark Juergensmeyer, *Terror in the Mind of God: The Global Rise of Religious Violence*, 4th edition (Berkeley: University of California Press, 2017), chapter 8; Mark Juergensmeyer, "Cosmic War," in John Barton, ed., *Oxford Research Encyclopedias: Religion* (New York: Oxford University Press, May 2016), http://religion.oxfordre.com/view/10.1093/acrefore/9780199340378.001.0001/acrefore-9780199340378-e-65.

20. Norman Cohn, *The Pursuit of the Millennium: Revolutionary Millenarians and Mystical Anarchists of the Middle Ages*, revised and expanded edition (1957; New York: Oxford University Press, 1970).

21. Meir Kahane, *Listen World, Listen Jew* (Jerusalem: Institute of the Jewish Idea, 1978), passim; Ehud Sprinzak, *The Ascendance of Israel's Radical Right* (New York: Oxford University Press, 1991).

22. Perry Schmidt-Leukel, *Religious Pluralism and Interreligious Theology* (Maryknoll, NY: Orbis Books, 2017), 190–193.

23. Author's interview with Abdul Aziz Rantisi, cofounder and political leader of Hamas, in Khan Yunis, Gaza, March 1, 1998.

24. Amarnath Amarasingam, "What Twitter Really Means for Islamic State Supporters," War on the Rocks, December 30, 2015, https://warontherocks.com/2015/12/what-twitter-really-means-for-islamic-state-supporters/.

5

Can Religion Cure War?

"DO YOU STILL believe in the peace process?" the teenage boy asked cynically. He posed the question to a former Muslim militant in the southern Philippine province of Mindanao, who described this incident to me when I was visiting Cotabato City, the main town of the region.[1] The former militant was now a lawyer and had renounced violence, but he continued to be a member of the separatist Moro Islamic Liberation Front. So he still considered himself an activist. But to the teenage son of a friend, he was not activist enough.

"What peace process is there?" the young man hissed. "Look at Marawi." He was referring to a nearby city that was described in the introductory chapter to this book, the one destroyed by the Philippine army in an attempt to rout a group of ISIS-affiliated militants who had taken the city and were holding it for ransom. Many Muslims in the region, including this teenager, blamed the army rather than ISIS for the destruction.

Days after their conversation, the lawyer told me, the boy disappeared. His family feared that he had joined the ISIS-affiliated rebels. The lawyer blamed himself for not doing more to persuade the young man that the peace process between the Muslim separatists and the Philippine government was still worthwhile. In fact in July 2018 President Rodrigo Duterte finally signed an agreement that had been negotiated four years before, but it was too late to save the teenager from joining the armed rebels.

"But would you have listened to this when you were his age?" I asked the lawyer, knowing about his past. He had joined the most militant branch of the separatist movement when he was in college and for years had fought against the forces of the Philippine government. He was engaged in a cosmic war between absolute enemies that resulted in violent encounters, guerrilla war, and a fifteen-year trail of bloodshed.

Why God Needs War and War Needs God. Mark Juergensmeyer, Oxford University Press (2020) © Oxford University Press. DOI: 10.1093/oso/9780190079178.001.0001

The lawyer smiled at my question, then started to tell me the story of how he had changed his point of view. In time he had begun to see the negotiations with the government as trustworthy.

"How did that happen?" I asked, wondering how he could turn from thinking in terms of cosmic war to civil engagement that could lead to a peace agreement.

It was as a student at Mindanao State University that he first became politically active. He was attracted to a Moro separatist movement that appeared tough and uncompromising, one that was militant and explicitly religious in its ideology. When he joined it, he felt that he was fighting for his faith, his community, his family, and himself.

It was a life-and-death struggle, he said. In his early days in the movement, he was willing to kill and die on behalf of its cause. He saw himself as a soldier in a righteous war, in a cosmic conflict of absolute right versus absolute wrong, against an enemy that did not deserve to live.

I asked him what changed, how he began to see the situation differently. His attitude about the need for self-government for Muslim Mindanao did not change, he said, but two things changed his attitude toward violence. One was simply the demands of domestic life. Later in his twenties he married and began to raise a family. He became busy with law school and an emerging career. Though he was no longer a combatant at this time, his basic outlook had not changed. He was still emotionally at war with the Philippine state and he supported armed resistance.

This view changed after he met a remarkable leader, Victor Corpus, a Philippine army official who had defected from the army, joined the Communist militants, and later returned to the army. He eventually became a general. When the lawyer met with him, the general had the credibility of someone who had been a rebel and reformed.

He understood us, the lawyer said. He could see how we would mistrust the government and want to embrace a new way of looking at politics. Yet he also was realistic. He could explain the futility of guerrilla warfare, and he told us how many of our goals could be met by negotiating a settlement.

When he and other Muslim separatist leaders accepted General Corpus's offer to arrange a meeting with government officials, the lawyer was surprised at how sensitive they were to the Muslim separatists' concerns. "They treated us with respect," he said.

This attitude of respect threw him off guard. It made it difficult to continue to see the other side as the evil enemy that deserved to be killed, and the image of intractable absolute war began to dissolve.

His story confirmed what I have heard from other former militants, from Christian militias in America to Buddhist extremists in Sri Lanka: the state of war is not necessarily a permanent condition. Just as people fall out of love or lose their faith in religion, they can also fall out of war. Or at least they can abandon the worldview of absolute war as a template for action in the world of everyday reality. In the case of the Mindanao lawyer, there was no suggestion that he had fundamentally changed his mind about the cosmic battle between good and evil. But he was no longer convinced that it was being played out in real time with real people. The general had treated him with respect. From that moment on it was hard to see him as a satanic foe. The idea of cosmic war had retreated to the realm of myth and symbol.

The lawyer's story of how war came to an end for him, or rather how the real-life enactment of an imagined reality of war ceased to be meaningful, may differ from the accounts of others who have abandoned the vision of war as it applied to real-life conflicts. But they often do abandon it. It is an alternative reality that is difficult to sustain over time.

The interesting thing is that ceasing to apply images of war to the real world does not necessarily mean abandoning the idea of war. War can continue in the mind long after it has left the battlefield. Though the idea of war might continue, this might be a satisfactory solution, for war in the mind doesn't kill people. If former militants are now playing war games on their computers or singing hymns about war in church, this doesn't bother most of us as long as they are not trying to do us in.

And in fact it may not be easy to rid the mind of war, even if we try. It seems to reside deep in the human psyche, a way of imagining an alternative reality that encompasses chaos. Even without being blessed by God, war is such a persistent element in the human imagination that it is hard to think of the world without it. Whenever people are under stress—as frequently people are—they are tempted to seek a different way of understanding the dilemma and its causes and to embrace the idea of an evil enemy against them. When whole societies are under stress, they may collectively see the world as engaged in war even if, as in the Cold War, the hostility seldom breaks out in actual military engagements. Often, of course, enemies are easy to imagine because they are indeed menacing. Like the Nazis in World War II, for example, they are opponents who want to change, punish, or destroy a society's public order. It is hardly a stretch of the imagination to see these foes in absolute terms, not merely as political rivals but as demonic creatures set on the annihilation of a people and their culture. By embracing an imagined view of the world at war, individuals find a resolution of these social tensions and clarification of the indecisive areas of their own lives. Hence the idea of war will always have a strong appeal on both social and personal levels. It will endure.

Is it possible to find a way to live with war? Is there a role for that other great alternative reality, religion, to play in ameliorating its effects?

Containing War

One way of dealing with war is to accept that military action is sometimes necessary to maintain justice in an unruly world. The idea here is to contain or redirect war and perhaps allow just a little bit of it in order to bring about a greater good. The ethical foundations of most religions have some version of what is known as the "just war theory" of conflict.[2] In Islam, the concept of jihad, frequently associated with the idea of holy war, also carries implications for the limitation of its use. According to the religious studies scholar John Kelsay, in undertaking jihad in a military sense (as opposed to simply striving for a more righteous life, which is what the word literally implies), a Muslim is limited by moral considerations regarding the purpose and the legitimacy of the undertaking.[3] This concept of jihad contains within it the main elements of the idea of a just war.

The principles of just war as it has evolved in the Western philosophic tradition are several. The reasons for war must be moral; it should be undertaken for a just cause. It should be approved by a legitimate governmental authority. It should be undertaken with a right intention and a reasonable chance of success. And it should be only a last resort, after all other means to resolve a conflict have been exhausted. Often the principle of proportionality is included among these requirements. This is the notion that the violence involved in resolving a conflict militarily should not be greater than the harm caused by the conflict itself. These principles are collectively known by the Latin phrase *jus ad bellum,* "rules before war." They are joined by another set of conditions governing the moral limitations of the conduct of warfare itself; these are known as *jus in bello,* "rules in war."

The idea of just war came to Christianity somewhat as an afterthought. Members of the early church tended to be pacifists. This was partly to resist being made to revere Caesar in a way that would imply that he had divinity or authority greater than religious authority. And it was partly in keeping with Christ's admonition to "turn the other cheek" (Matthew 5:38–40). It is hard to live by the teachings of Jesus's Sermon on the Mount and support war (Matthew 5:1–12).

But when Christianity became the state religion of the Roman Empire after the conversion of the Emperor Constantine in 312, Christian thinkers tried to reconcile the pacifist mandate of the New Testament with the need to morally justify the military actions of the state. They tried to accommodate the idea of defensive war within the nonviolent idealism of the Gospels in a way that would not glorify bloodshed.

The fourth-century theologian Augustine of Hippo hit upon a solution. Augustine expanded on the concept of "just war" developed by Cicero in Roman jurisprudence and set it into context. The perfect ethic of peace that Jesus talked about, he reasoned, was appropriate to the "city of God," to which we should all aspire.[4] We live, however, in a more mundane realm—the "city of man"—where life is less pleasant and force is sometimes necessary to keep evil at bay. Augustine specified the conditions in which a Christian could morally sanction war. He condemned "the lust for power" as an inappropriate reason for warfare. These conditions were later refined by the medieval theologian Thomas Aquinas and have become the bedrock of the church's teaching on the morality of war ever since.

Contemporary Christian thinking continues to be guided by just war criteria. One of the twentieth century's most influential Protestant thinkers, Reinhold Niebuhr, began his career as a pacifist and then grudgingly accepted the role of the military in preserving order and justice. The actions of Hitler and Stalin persuaded Niebuhr that there were moments when evil had to be countered by military force for justice to prevail. As I have mentioned earlier in this book, in his influential essay, *Why the Christian Church Is Not Pacifist*, Niebuhr cited the Christian tradition that the defense of justice is more important than pacifism when it comes to great encounters between evil powers and social order.

The idea of just war allows religion to approve of certain forms of military action. This is a reasonable moral calculation regarding the necessity of police and soldiers in maintaining order and achieving justice. But it focuses solely on the application of military force. It does not deal with the idea of war. One can entertain the notion of a cosmic encounter and at the same time accept the limitations of just war, I suppose, though the two are not really compatible. It is hard to imagine a jihadi warrior inspired by the apocalyptic ideology of the Islamic State charging into battle and then suddenly stopping to check whether he and his colleagues have been morally approved by a legitimate authority and were motivated by a right intention. Similarly it is unlikely that the Christian militia soldier who believes in the end-times apocalypse will check to make sure his battles are in line with proportionality and undertaken for a just cause.

Though, come to think of it, an abortion clinic bomber has done just that. Rev. Michael Bray, a Christian militant convicted of attacking abortion centers, once told me that his actions were in accord with the principle of just war since he was applying only a small amount of violence to counter the thousands of lives that, in his calculation, were immorally cut short by abortion.[5] Still, I think he may have just been trying to impress me, showing that he could play my game by coming up with rational reasons for his actions within traditional ethical frameworks. I suspect that his real motivation may have been rooted in a vision of cosmic war and an absolute battle with the forces of secularism. Just war is not easily reconciled with this kind of militant absolutism, I'm afraid.

War without Blood

The concept of just war may be the best way to limit warfare once a party is determined to undertake it, but it is worth pondering whether it is possible to avert war from ever becoming a reality in the first place. Or, to put it another way, since the idea of war is just that, an idea, is it possible to have war without bloodshed? What I have in mind are ways to conceive of war, even cosmic war, without actually having to fight it. The idea is to keep war on a symbolic level, and this is an arena in which literature, video games, and religion might be helpful allies.

According to Freud, violent religious symbols and sacrificial rituals evoke, and in the process vent, violent impulses. Freud was concerned with individual tendencies toward violence rather than large-scale socially promoted ones, like warfare, but the mechanism of symbolically displacing violence could work on both the personal and the social scale. Freud found inspiration for his theories in the persistence of the ancient Greek myth in which the king of Thebes, Oedipus, accidentally fulfills a prophecy that he would kill his father and sleep with his mother. What interested Freud about this tale of accidental patricide and maternal incest was its endurance over the years. The reason for its popularity, he speculated, is that it vicariously allows those men who tell it to project onto it their own desire to kill their father and have sex with their mother, and thus symbolically displace the need to do either. This theory, first discussed in *The Interpretation of Dreams,* was later developed in *Totem and Taboo,* where Freud argued that the Christian ritual of the Eucharist is a kind of acting out of the Oedipus myth, allowing the faithful to participate symbolically in the death of Jesus, the father figure of Christianity.

The literary theorist René Girard has updated Freud's insight in a way that makes it relevant to how we think about war. In Girard's view, ritualized violence—including the glorification of mythic wars—can help to symbolically defuse a potentially tragic encounter. He explains that societies have devised cultural dams to prevent the rivalry between competitors from overflowing into violence. One such cultural institution is religion, which shelters the expression of cathartic violence in the guise of ritualized sacrifice. Through religion, Girard claims, the death of a sacrificial victim becomes a saving death, and the scapegoat who is the symbolic butt of the violence is celebrated as a cultural hero. In Girard's reckoning, by enhancing the role of religion in providing symbolic releases for violent passions the possibility of real violence can be reduced: "The function of ritual is to 'purify' violence; that is, to 'trick' violence into spending itself on victims whose death will provoke no reprisals."[6]

According to Girard, this is the function of sacrifice, including symbolic sacrifice, in religious ritual; it displaces real aggression with a symbolic enactment of it. This becomes relevant in thinking about war when one considers that war can be thought of as a reciprocity between sacrifice and martyrdom: sacrificing members of the enemy's side and raising up martyrs on one's own. Behind the gruesome litany of sacrifice and martyrdom is something that encompasses both and much more: the idea of cosmic war played out in symbolic narration. The depiction of cosmic war in myth and ritual is a way of displacing the urge to participate in a real war. The gorier the imagined battle, the more heroic and victorious the fictional triumph, the more satisfying are these images of cosmic war. And thus, so the theory goes, there is less need to engage in the more limited forms of actual war.

Does this really work? Maybe. There are studies that attempt to measure empirically whether, for example, obsession with violent video games lessens the aggression that leads to real violence or whether instead it stokes aggression. The popular assumption is that such games lead to real acts of violence and should be banned or, at the very least, controlled. The theories of Freud and Girard, on the other hand, suggest that they might actually help to ameliorate violence. Which is the case? A longitudinal study reported in the Molecular Psychiatry section of the journal *Nature* in 2018 arrived at an interesting conclusion: there was no effect at all.[7] Two groups of subjects played two kinds of video games, one violent (Grand Theft Auto) and one nonviolent (involving Sims-style role-playing). After giving players a battery of tests meant to discern changes in empathy, aggression, and interpersonal cooperation, the scientists found no difference between the two groups. This does not conclusively prove that the ideas of Freud and Girard are baseless, but it does raise questions as to whether displacing violence onto symbols really works.

There are other ways in which we can participate in a war-like situation without actually engaging in violent conflict or killing people. One is to use the idea of war metaphorically. The "war on poverty" and the "war on drugs" are two examples. But most people probably regard these as mere figures of speech and do not take them as seriously as one would an engagement in a real war.

Someone who advocated taking nonviolent war seriously was Mohandas Gandhi. In Gandhi's reckoning the war against injustice requires all the discipline and commitment of soldiers engaged in battle. This was real war, in his calculation. He thought of social conflict as the struggle to move toward *satyagraha*, "truth force" or "grasping after truth." To engage in it involved direct confrontation between clashing points of view and the people who defended them—battles that could be fierce and potentially violent. But the violence would not come from Gandhi's troops, whom he called *satyagrahis*. They would be trained in as disciplined a manner as soldiers preparing for a military expedition. They would learn how to bear the brunt of violence rather than be the instruments of it. When Gandhi led his *satyagrahis* in skirmishes with the British army over the right of Indians to purify their own salt for domestic purposes, they had disciplined themselves to accept violence and not fight back. But they were engaged in a war-like struggle all the same.

Gandhi developed his ideas about nonviolent warfare in resisting racist policies in South Africa, where he led a movement of Indian immigrants. But his thinking about war began even earlier, in his reading of the classic Hindu epic the *Mahabharata*, especially the part we have discussed earlier, the *Bhagavad Gita*, in which Lord Krishna explains to Arjuna why he has no choice but to enter the field of battle in a fierce war between two sets of cousins. He cannot escape this turmoil, so the only question is how to deal with it. Lord Krishna suggests that one should seek to perfect the art of struggling without passion, dealing with life's unavoidable battles honorably and graciously rather than trying to win them. Winning is, in any event, ultimately futile.

This leads to the notion of "nonattached action," the idea that one should fight virtuously rather than trying to win by any means necessary. Gandhi discovered this idea in the *Bhagavad Gita* as a student in London, when he was asked to lead a discussion on the meaning of this most popular of the Hindu scriptures.[8] The lesson stuck with the young man, and later in life he applied it in political struggles, first in South Africa and then in India, where he molded the concept of nonattached action into the strategy of nonviolent conflict that he called *satyagraha*. Gandhi thus found a way of redirecting war into a different kind of struggle: the struggle for truth.

Although *satyagraha* is often described as a means of conflict resolution, it is basically a theory of conflict. Gandhi was fascinated with the idea of conflict and saw it as a way of broadening one's view of the truth. He insisted that in any clash it was necessary to look beyond personal differences to the larger issues behind each side. Every conflict, Gandhi reasoned, was a contestation on two levels: between persons and between principles. Behind every fighter was the issue for which the fighter was fighting. Every fight was on some level an encounter between differing "angles of vision" illuminating the same truth.[9] It was this difference— sometimes a difference in worldviews—that must be resolved in order for a fight to be ended and the fighters reconciled. Gandhi's methods were more than a way of confronting an enemy; they were a way of dealing with conflict itself.

One could undertake a war on poverty or a war against injustice as a real war in a Gandhian sense, as something more than metaphor. It could be a way of acting out warfare in nonviolent terms. Though it is not an overtly religious approach, it is compatible with religious ideals and has been championed by various religious leaders. It is no surprise that the civil rights martyr Rev. Martin Luther King Jr. traveled to India to study Gandhian ideas and methods before embarking on his own nonviolent campaign for the civil rights of all Americans. One could imagine, then, that the urge to war could be fulfilled nonviolently in ethical confrontations over vital public issues. The lawyer I met in Mindanao might still be engaged in a great struggle for the rights of his Muslim coreligionists, even though he is not taking up weapons or intending to cause bloodshed. But perhaps in his mind it is war all the same.

Living with Competing Realities

Let me finish my story about the Filipino lawyer who had gradually abandoned the idea of cosmic war. I have said that he continues to be committed to the cause of justice for Muslims in the region. He helped to negotiate a peace agreement that guarantees their full political participation in public life and full access to government benefits. In working out the implementation of the agreement after it was signed by President Duterte in July 2018, he continues the struggle. So in that sense he is still engaged in a struggle for justice, a kind of nonviolent war.

What I have not mentioned is the religious awakening that he has experienced in recent years. Increasingly, he told me, his Muslim faith has become a more vital part of his personal life. He prays regularly, he goes to the mosque weekly, he participates in all the major holidays, and he is attempting to raise his children on a virtuous path. Part of this increased religiosity, I suspect, comes with age and responsibility. As individuals move from youth to middle age, many turn to traditional social and cultural institutions for support and to share the responsibility of ethical mentorship for their children.

But I sensed that in his case it was more than that. He seemed eager for me to know about this aspect of his life these days. I asked him whether it has replaced his earlier commitment to the cosmic war of battle against the government. He paused before answering, as if he had not entertained this idea before. "Perhaps," he said. "For whatever reason, it is real."

The Muslim lawyer has made an accommodation between war and religion. At one time the two realities were fused in an image of cosmic war, a righteous battle in which bloodshed was expected and no holds were barred. Today he sees the world differently. War and religion continue to be a real part of his life, but not in the form of cosmic war. He keeps them separate, as alternative ways of thinking about the world and being in it that do not prevent him from engaging fully in ordinary civil society.

I suspect that his way of dealing with these two great alternative realities, war and religion, is not uncommon. There are, as Robert Bellah observed, multiple realities that can overlap. One does not have to choose one or the other. One can live in a world in which a war mentality exists and not let it consume you, and where religious realities exist and not let them devour you. Of course some people will go to the religious and bellicose extremes, but for many of us the temperate way of dealing with alternative realities is to accept them as just that, alternatives that can illuminate facets of daily life without overwhelming them.

At the beginning of the twentieth century, H. G. Wells wrote a pamphlet encouraging the British to engage the Germans in a "war to end war." The phrase was picked up by US President Woodrow Wilson, with whom it is widely associated and often repeated as evidence of his naiveté. World War I most certainly did not end war; World War II was far more costly in lives and set the stage for what was de facto the third world war of the twentieth century, the Cold War. Nor do the wars of the twenty-first century hold the promise of ending all wars in the future, and no one dares to suggest that they might be. War, it seems, is with us for all time. The war worldview, in which chaos is conquered through cosmic battles between good and evil, is perversely attractive. We are strangely drawn to the idea of war, both real war and perhaps even more so the wars of our imagination. The flood of images of imagined wars in movies and novels and video games seems to be an unending torrent. As a species, we humans seem to need war.

We also seem to need religion. Marx may have predicted that religion would wither away, and some theologians of the secular 1950s and 1960s may have announced that God was dead, at least in a traditional sense. But God seems to have come back to life in the twenty-first century. The percentage of believers in Europe and the United States continues to decline, but the expression of their belief is more public and outgoing than before, and in the rest of the world belief flourishes. The religious imagination continues to thrive.

So these great alternative realities, war and religion, continue to exist as part of our cultural creativity and social striving. But we need not succumb to the temptation of thinking solely in terms of either religion or war. And even those who do persist in thinking in these ways can be tolerated, as long as they do not act out their imagined realities and force them on us. If our next-door neighbors are obsessed with a certain set of extreme religious beliefs, we can regard them as peculiar or pathetic if we wish, but unless they demand that we follow those beliefs or act in a way that disturbs our peace, we are not bothered by them. In the same way we can abide militants committed to war realities as long as they keep it to themselves and do not build bombs in their bathrooms or harass the neighbors.

In other words, we can acknowledge that people are capable of living with multiple realities and still get along in the world. Cultural traditions from literature to religion enshrine images of warfare without encouraging anyone to act on those ways of thinking. Fortunately we are still united, most of us, in the reality of everyday civil order. These alternative realities may challenge and fascinate the mind. Whether we adopt them fully and make them dominant in a way that determines our actions and disturbs the tranquility of others is a calculation that each person has to make. We can either control them or succumb to them. The choice is ours.

It is possible to abide the violent images of war as long as they stay in the realm of the cultural imagination. In an interesting way, then, perhaps the cure for the horrors of war is religion. When the alternative reality of religion encompasses a conflict of ultimate values on a transcendent plane, this imagined warfare can excite human creativity without destroying it. Humans will always imagine war and will always imagine religion; perhaps these are the most creative acts of human consciousness, to envision such extraordinary reaches of cosmic confrontation and to pose such dramatic alternatives to everyday reality as war and religion provide. But it is also within the creative power of the species to think reasonably about differences and profoundly respect the sanctity of life. Perhaps this latter impulse will eventually be war's captain and humanity's saving grace.

Notes

1. Interview with the author, Cotabato City, Mindanao, Philippines, April 3, 2018.
2. Paul Robinson, ed., *Just War in Comparative Perspective* (London: Routledge, 2003).
3. John Kelsay, *Arguing the Just War in Islam* (Cambridge MA: Harvard University Press, 2009).
4. Augustine of Hippo, *The City of God*, trans. Henry Bettenson (London: Penguin Books, 2016).
5. Author's interview with Michael Bray, pastor, Reformation Lutheran Church, and editor of *Capitol Area Christian News*, Bowie, Maryland, April 25, 1996.
6. René Girard, *Violence and the Sacred*, trans. Patrick Gregory (Baltimore, MD: Johns Hopkins University Press, 1972), 36.
7. Simone Kühn, Dimitrij Tycho Kugler, Katharina Schmalen, Markus Weichenberger, Charlotte Witt, and Jürgen Gallinat, "Does Playing Violent Video Games Cause Aggression? A Longitudinal Intervention Study," *Nature*, March 13, 2018, https://www.nature.com/articles/s41380-018-0031-7.
8. I discuss this incident in Gandhi's life in Mark Juergensmeyer, "Gandhi vs. Terrorism," *Daedalus* 136.1 (Winter 2007): 30–39.
9. Gandhi, writing in *Young India*, September 23, 1926 . I explore Gandhi's ideas further in Mark Juergensmeyer, *Gandhi's Way: A Handbook of Conflict Resolution*, revised edition (Berkeley: University of California Press, 2005.

Selected Bibliography

Amarasingam, Amarnath. "What Twitter Really Means for Islamic State Supporters." War on the Rocks, December 30, 2015. https://warontherocks.com/2015/12/what-twitter-really-means-for-islamic-state-supporters/.

Armstrong, Karen. *Fields of Blood: Religion and the History of Violence.* New York: Knopf, 2014.

Armstrong, Rebecca. "Jihad: Play the Game." *The Independent,* August 17, 2005. https://www.independent.co.uk/news/science/jihad-play-the-game-5347294.html.

Asad, Talal. *Geneologies of Religion: Discipline and Reasons of Power in Christianity and Islam.* Baltimore, MD: Johns Hopkins University Press, 1993.

Asad, Talal. "Reading a Modern Classic: Wilfred Cantwell Smith's *The Meaning and End of Religion.*" *History of Religions* 40 (2001): 205–222.

Aslan, Reza. "Cosmic War in Religious Traditions." In Mark Juergensmeyer, Margo Kitts, and Michael Jerryson, eds., *The Oxford Handbook of Religion and Violence.* New York: Oxford University Press, 2014, 260–267.

Aslan, Reza. *How to Win a Cosmic War: Confronting Radical Religions.* New York: Arrow, 2010.

Atwan, Abdel Bari. *Islamic State: The Digital Caliphate.* Berkeley: University of California Press, 2015.

Augustine of Hippo. *The City of God.* Trans. Henry Bettenson. London: Penguin Books, 2016.

Avalos, Hector. *Fighting Words: The Origins of Religious Violence.* New York: Prometheus Books, 2005.

Becker, Ernest. *The Denial of Death.* New York: Simon and Schuster, 1973.

Bellah, Robert Neely. *Religion in Human Evolution: From the Paleolithic to the Axial Age.* Cambridge, MA: Harvard University Press, 2011.

Berger, Peter, and Thomas Luckmann. *The Social Construction of Reality: A Treatise in the Sociology of Knowledge.* New York: Penguin Random House, 1966.

bin Laden, Osama. "Declaration of Jihad." Trans. James Howarth. In Bruce Lawrence, ed., *Messages to the World: The Statements of Osama bin Laden*. London: Verso, 2005, 30.

Blin, Arnaud. *War and Religion: Europe and the Mediterranean from the First through the Twenty-First Century*. Oakland: University of California Press, 2019.

Bloch, Maurice. *Prey into Hunter*. Cambridge, UK: Cambridge University Press, 1992.

Bonhoeffer, Dietrich. *Letters and Papers from Prison*. Ed. Eberhard Bethge. New York: Simon and Schuster Touchstone Books, 1997. Originally published as *Widerstand und Ergebung: Briefe und Aufzeichnungen aus der Haft*. Munich: Christian Kaiser Verlag, 1970.

Burkert, Walter. *Homo Necans: The Anthropology of Ancient Greek Sacrificial Ritual and Myth*. Trans. Peter Bing. Berkeley: University of California Press, 1972.

Burkhert, Walter, Rene Girard, and Jonathan Z. Smith. *Violent Origins: Ritual Killing and Cultural Formation*. Ed. Robert G. Hamerton-Kelly. Stanford, CA: Stanford University Press, 1987.

Caillois, Roger. *Bellone ou la Pente de la Guerre*. Paris: Flammarion, 2012.

Chapman, Stephen. "Martial Memory, Peaceable Vision." In Heath Thomas, Jeremy Evans, and Paul Copan, eds., *Holy War in the Bible*. Downers Grove, IL: InterVarsity Press, 2013, 122–134.

Clausewitz, Carl von. *On War*. 1832. Trans. Michael Howard and Peter Paret. Princeton, NJ: Princeton University Press, 1984.

Cohn, Norman. *The Pursuit of the Millennium: Revolutionary Millenarians and Mystical Anarchists of the Middle Ages*. 1957. Revised and expanded edition. New York: Oxford University Press, 1970.

Crabtree, Harriet. *The Christian Life: Traditional Metaphors and Contemporary Theologies*. Minneapolis, MN: Fortress Press, Harvard Dissertations in Religion, 1991.

Dawkins, Richard. *The God Delusion*. New York: Mariner Books, 2006.

Denton-Borhaug, Kelly. *US War–Culture, Sacrifice and Salvation*. London: Routledge, 2014.

Filkins, Dexter. "What Do They Want? Graeme Wood Speaks with Supporters of ISIS." *New York Times*, January 19, 2017.

Fox, Robin. "Fatal Attraction: War and Human Nature." *National Interest*, no. 30 (Winter 1992–1993): 11–20.

Gelven, Michael. *War and Existence: A Philosophical Inquiry*. University Park: Pennsylvania State University Press, 1994.

Girard, René. *The Scapegoat*. Trans. Yvonne Freccero. Baltimore, MD: Johns Hopkins University Press, 1986.

Girard, René. *Violence and the Sacred*. Trans. Patrick Gregory. Baltimore, MD: Johns Hopkins University Press, 1977.

Harris, Sam. *The End of Faith: Religion, Terror, and the Future of Reason*. New York: Norton, 2005.

Hashmi, Sohail H. *Just Wars, Holy Wars, and Jihads: Christian, Jewish, and Muslim Encounters and Exchanges.* New York: Oxford University Press, 2012.

Hassner, Ron E. *War on Sacred Grounds.* Ithaca, NY: Cornell University Press, 2009.

Hedges, Christopher. *War Is a Force That Gives Us Meaning.* New York: Anchor Books, 2002.

Hegghammer, Thomas. *Jihadi Culture: The Art and Social Practices of Militant Islamicists.* Cambridge, UK: Cambridge University Press, 2017.

Hemingway, Ernst. *For Whom the Bell Tolls.* New York: Charles Scribner's Sons, 1940.

Hillman, James. *A Terrible Love of War.* New York: Penguin Books, 2005.

Huizinga, Johan. *Homo Ludens: A Study of the Play-Element in Culture.* 1944. London: Routledge, 1949.

Huntington, Samuel. "The Clash of Civilizations?" *Foreign Affairs* 72.3 (Summer 1993): 22–49.

James, William. *The Varieties of Religious Experience.* 1902. New York: Penguin Classics, 1985.

Johnson, James Turner. *The Holy War Idea in Western and Islamic Traditions.* University Park: Pennsylvania State University Press, 1997.

Juergensmeyer, Mark. "Chatting with Myanmar's Buddhist Terrorist." *Religion Dispatches,* February 17, 2015.

Juergensmeyer, Mark. "Cosmic War." In John Barton, ed., *Oxford Research Encyclopedias: Religion.* New York: Oxford University Press, May 2016. http://religion.oxfordre.com/view/10.1093/acrefore/9780199340378.001.0001/acrefore-9780199340378-e-65.

Juergensmeyer, Mark. *Gandhi's Way: A Handbook of Conflict Resolution.* Revised edition. Berkeley: University of California Press, 2005.

Juergensmeyer, Mark. "Gandhi vs. Terrorism." *Daedalus* 136.1 (Winter 2007): 30–39.

Juergensmeyer, Mark. *Global Rebellion: Religious Challenges to the Secular State.* Berkeley: University of California Press, 2008.

Juergensmeyer, Mark. *Terror in the Mind of God: The Global Rise of Religious Violence.* 4th edition. Berkeley: University of California Press, 2017.

Kahane, Meir. *Listen World, Listen Jew.* Jerusalem: Institute of the Jewish Idea, 1978.

Kelsay, John. *Arguing the Just War in Islam.* Cambridge, MA: Harvard University Press, 2009.

Kitts, Margo. "Ancient Near Eastern Perspectives on Evil and Terror." In Chad Meister and Paul Moser, eds., *Cambridge Companion to the Problem of Evil.* Cambridge, UK: Cambridge University Press, 2016, 165–192.

Kitts, Margo. "The Near Eastern Chaoskampf in the River-Battle of Iliad 21." *Journal of Ancient Near Eastern Religions* 13.1 (2013): 86–112.

Koenigsberg, Richard. *Hitler's Holocaust: The Logic of War and Genocide.* Amazon Digital Services, Library of Social Science, 2018.

Kühn, Simone, Dimitrij Tycho Kugler, Katharina Schmalen, Markus Weichenberger, Charlotte Witt, and Jürgen Gallinat. "Does Playing Violent Video Games Cause

Aggression? A Longitudinal Intervention Study." *Nature*, March 13, 2018. https://www.nature.com/articles/s41380-018-0031-7.

LaBarre, Weston. *The Ghost Dance: Origins of Religion*. London: Allen and Unwin, 1972.

LaHaye, Tim, and Jerry B. Jenkins. *Left Behind: A Novel of the Earth's Last Days*. Carol Stream, IL: Tyndale House, 1995.

Lakomy, Miron. "Let's Play a Video Game: *Jihadi* Propaganda in the World of Electronic Entertainment." *Studies in Conflict and Terrorism Journal*, October 23, 2017. https://www.tandfonline.com/doi/abs/10.1080/1057610X.2017.1385903.

Lewis, Bernard. "The Roots of Muslim Rage." *New Republic*, September 1990.

Lind, M. C. *Yahweh Is a Warrior: The Theology of Warfare in Ancient Israel*. Scottsdale, AZ: Herald Press, 1980.

Ludendorff, Erich. *Der Totale Krieg*. Munich: Ludendorffs Verlag, 1936.

Mansfield, Stephen. *The Faith of the American Soldier*. New York: Penguin, 2005.

Marguesee, Mike. "A Name That Lives in Infamy," *The Guardian Website*, November 10, 2005. https://www.theguardian.com/world/2005/nov/10/usa.iraq.

McAlister, Melani. "An Empire of Their Own." *The Nation*, September 22, 2003.

McCants, William. *The ISIS Apocalypse: The History, Strategy and Doomsday Vision of the Islamic State*. New York: St. Martin's Press, 2015.

Miller, Randall M., Harry S. Stout, and Charles Reagan Wilson, eds. *Religion and the American Civil War*. New York: Oxford University Press, 1998.

Murphy, Tim. "Oh Magog! Why End-Time Buffs Are Freaking Out about Syria." *Mother Jones*, September 4, 2013.

Niebuhr, Reinhold. *Why the Christian Church Is Not Pacifist*. London: Student Christian Movement Press, 1940.

Palmer-Fernandez, Gabriel, ed. *Encyclopedia of Religion and War*. London: Routledge, 2004.

Partner, Peter. *God of Battles: Holy Wars of Christianity and Islam*. Princeton, NJ: Princeton University Press, 1997.

Pettigrew, Joyce. *The Sikhs of the Punjab: Unheard Voices of State and Guerilla Violence*. London: Zed Books, 1995.

Puri, Harish K., Paramjit Singh Judge, and Jagrup Singh Sekhon. *Terrorism in Punjab: Understanding Grassroots Reality*. New Delhi: Har-Anand Publications, 1999.

Robinson, Paul, ed. *Just War in Comparative Perspective*. London: Routledge, 2003.

Rosenberg, Joel. "My Spiritual Journey." Joel Rosenberg Website. Accessed July 22, 2018. https://www.joelrosenberg.com/my-spiritual-journey/.

Sagan, Eli. *Cannibalism: Human Aggression and Cultural Form*. New York: Psychohistory Press, 1974.

Sagan, Eli. *The Lust to Annihilate: A Psychoanalytic Study of Violence in Ancient Greek Culture*. New York: Psychohistory Press, 1972.

Schmidt-Leukel, Perry. *Religious Pluralism and Interreligious Theology*. Maryknoll, NY: Orbis Books, 2017.

Schütz, Alfred. *Phenomenology of the Social World.* Trans. George Walsh. Evanston, IL: Northwestern University Press, 1967.

Sheikh, Mona Kanwal. *Guardians of God: Inside the Religious Mind of the Pakistani Taliban.* New Delhi: Oxford University Press, 2016.

Smend, R. S. *Yahweh War and Tribal Confederation.* Trans. M. G. Rogers. Nashville, TN: Abingdon Press, 1970.

Smith, Wilfred Cantwell. *The Meaning and End of Religion: A New Approach.* New York: Charles Scribner's Sons, 1962.

Sprinzak, Ehud. *The Ascendance of Israel's Radical Right.* New York: Oxford University Press, 1991.

Staal, J. Frits. *Agni: The Vedic Ritual of the Fire Altar.* Berkeley, CA: Asian Humanities Press, 1983.

Stoessinger, John. *Why Nations Go to War.* 1974. 11th edition. Belmont, CA: Wadsworth, 2010.

Stout, Harry S. *Upon the Altar of the Nation: A Moral History of the Civil War.* New York: Viking, 2006.

Svennson, Isak. *Ending Holy Wars: Religion and Conflict Resolution in Civil Wars.* St. Lucia: University of Queensland Press, 2012.

Taylor, Charles. *A Secular Age.* Cambridge, MA: Harvard University Press, 2007.

Von Rad, Gerhard. *Holy War in Ancient Israel.* 1952. Trans. John Yoder and Marva Dawn. Grand Rapids, MI: Eerdman's, 1996.

Wallis, Arthur. *Battle: A Manual of Christian Life.* New York: Harper, 1973.

Waltz, Kenneth. *Man, the State, and War: A Theoretical Analysis.* New York: Columbia University Press, 1959.

Walzer, Michael. *Arguing about War.* New Haven, CT: Yale University Press, 2004.

Wood, Graeme. "Three Types of ISIS Fighters." *New Republic,* September 10, 2014.

Wood, Graeme. *The Way of the Strangers: Encounters with the Islamic State.* New York: Random House, 2017.

Wood, Graeme. "What ISIS Really Wants." *The Atlantic,* March 2015.

Woodward, Bob. *Bush at War.* New York: Simon and Schuster, 2002.

Woodward, Steven E. *While God Is Marching On: The Religious World of Civil War Soldiers.* Lawrence: University of Kansas Press, 2001.

Index

For the benefit of digital users, indexed terms that span two pages (e.g., 52–53) may, on occasion, appear on only one of those pages.